1939 – The Coming of the Storm

Middlesbrough and the surrounding communities were a hub of vital wartime industries. Middlesbrough was home to iron and steel works, a large petrochemical industry along with chemical works, while the massive ICI plant at Billingham was of crucial national importance. The largely redundant ironstone mines of Cleveland also received a temporary boost due to the war, while the shipyards at South Bank and Stockton were also of national importance.

The British government anticipated that the start of the war would be marked with concentrated bombing attacks on industrial centres and had put wide-ranging plans in place to counteract and alleviate this. A nationwide system of Air Raid Precautions (ARP) was put in place which were organised and run by local councils and were therefore rather ad-hoc with variations in training, enthusiasm, levels of manning and competence, and leadership. The average ARP scheme was run by officers selected by the council's watch committee or emergency committee and in a large number of cases this responsibility fell to the chair, or his deputy, of the committee, or a prominent local figure such as the chief constable of the local police force. While this made sense from an organisational perspective it could often cause resentment among the more junior officers who served in various aspects of an area's ARP scheme. It was also open to corruption and incompetence.

The actual manning of an ARP scheme required a large number of people in a bewildering number of roles. At the very least there had to be a sufficient number of ARP wardens whose duties included patrolling the streets during alerts, checking blackouts, inspecting air raid shelters, helping the emergency services and controlling people during air raid alerts. Next were the men of the rescue squads.

These were usually split into light and heavy units and consisted of men who were experienced in manual labour, often in the building trade or from some council roles, and were physically fit. Their duties in the event of a raid were arduous in that they were expected to not only clear rubble and debris, but also to rescue those who had been trapped and to recover bodies; many witnessed sights which would haunt them. First aid and medical posts also had to be manned by trained and enthusiastic volunteers while there was also a pressing need for stretcher bearers and ambulance drivers. Others were expected to establish and staff rest and feeding centres which would be opened in the event of raiding (often in local schools which had been commandeered for the purpose). Other more specialised teams were created to handle the dangers of chemical attack. It was widely feared that gas bombs would be utilised and so gas and decontamination squads were an integral part of any ARP scheme. These were usually manned by trained chemists and men and women from the council's public works departments. The Auxiliary Fire Service (AFS) was another key part of any planning for ARP. The AFS consisted of volunteers who were trained in rudimentary fire-fighting techniques and who would be expected to support the local brigades in the event of raids. The AFS and the local brigades were later rolled into the National Fire Service (NFS) in 1941. In addition to all of these services were a myriad of other smaller groups of ARP workers. The ARP services also required a vast administrative network which employed even more people. Leadership, clerical roles, stores and other functions all had to be managed if an ARP scheme was to be effective.

One of the biggest problems facing the various ARP services was the lack of sufficient motor vehicles. As a result, when war broke out all manner of vehicles, many of which would otherwise have been laid up due to petrol rationing, were commandeered or volunteered for service with the ARP. Mr Stanley Haggath had joined he AFS in South Bank a year before war broke out and at the start of the war he found himself appointed as section officer in charge of an area including Normanby, South Bank, and Teesville. For equipment, his section had

YOUR TOWNS & CITIES IN WORLD WAR TWO

MIDDLESBROUGH

AT WAR 1939–45

For My Parents

YOUR TOWNS & CITIES IN WORLD WAR TWO

MIDDLESBROUGH

AT WAR 1939–45

CRAIG ARMSTRONG

Pen & Sword
MILITARY
AN IMPRINT OF PEN & SWORD BOOKS LTD.
YORKSHIRE · PHILADELPHIA

First published in Great Britain in 2022 by
Pen & Sword Military
an imprint of
Pen & Sword Books Ltd
Yorkshire – Philadelphia

Copyright © Craig Armstrong, 2022

ISBN 978 1 52670 476 4

The right of Craig Armstrong to be identified as Author of this work has been
asserted by him in accordance with the Copyright, Designs and Patents Act 1988.

A CIP catalogue record for this book is
available from the British Library.

All rights reserved. No part of this book may be reproduced or transmitted in any
form or by any means, electronic or mechanical including photocopying, recording
or by any information storage and retrieval system, without permission from the
Publisher in writing.

Typeset by SJmagic DESIGN SERVICES, India.
Printed and bound in the UK by CPI Group (UK) Ltd, Croydon, CR0 4YY.

Pen & Sword Books Limited incorporates the imprints of Atlas, Archaeology,
Aviation, Discovery, Family History, Fiction, History, Maritime, Military, Military
Classics, Politics, Select, Transport, True Crime, Air World, Frontline Publishing,
Leo Cooper, Remember When, Seaforth Publishing, The Praetorian Press,
Wharncliffe Local History, Wharncliffe Transport, Wharncliffe True Crime and
White Owl.

For a complete list of Pen & Sword titles please contact
PEN & SWORD BOOKS LIMITED
47 Church Street, Barnsley, South Yorkshire, S70 2AS, England
E-mail: enquiries@pen-and-sword.co.uk
Website: www.pen-and-sword.co.uk

Or
PEN AND SWORD BOOKS
1950 Lawrence Rd, Havertown, PA 19083, USA
E-mail: Uspen-and-sword@casematepublishers.com
Website: www.penandswordbooks.com

Contents

a light trailer-mounted pump towed by a baker's van. Mr Haggath had previously worked for the bakery as a driver and salesman.

In Middlesbrough there were some unusual aspects in the formation and running of the ARP scheme. In 1938 then Councillor (later Sir) William Crosthwaite urged the council to appoint a special committee responsible for ARP. His suggestion was not only approved but the council also allowed Crosthwaite, at his request, to select the membership of the committee himself. He selected two Aldermen (John Wesley Brown and Emmanuel Spencer) and four fellow Councillors (T.K. Briggs, R.V.C. Gray, Tom Meehan, and John W. Welch) to sit on the committee alongside himself as chair. The committee had wide-ranging duties to oversee including all of those mentioned above, plus nursing services, provision and management of air raid shelters, evacuation and billeting, information provision services, and war damage repairs. In September and October 1939 the committee met on a daily basis, but on 5 September it had to accept a government instruction that the Town Clerk, Mr Preston Kitchen, be appointed as ARP Controller, meaning that Councillor Crosthwaite was acting in a deputy (albeit very influential) role, but remained as chair of the committee. Throughout the rest of the war the committee met at least once per month with additional meetings as emergency dictated. By the end of the war in Europe it had met on more than 130 occasions.

One of the greatest challenges facing the committee, and one which had to be organised well in advance of war, requiring a large logistical effort, was the planning and provision of air raid shelters for the population of Middlesbrough. It was initially proposed that a capacity of 100,000 should be provided. This was a massive undertaking and involved the surveying of sites and the establishment of priorities. Shelters were to consist of simple trench shelters (largely dug in parks and on wasteland), surface shelters constructed of brick, concrete and steel to be placed in high-population areas where individual Anderson shelters were largely impracticable, school shelters for the 19,000 children in the town (evacuation notwithstanding), and shelters to be constructed in the basements of commercial properties (which required requisitioning using the raft of emergency powers granted by the government). Other properties were purchased. Among these was the vicar's residence at St Aidan's Lodge in Linthorpe Road which was bought so that it could be used as a centre for the training of ARP personnel in anti-gas techniques.

In Stockton the provision of shelters for the children of Holy Trinity School led to an incident which horrified the headmaster. At first the school was assigned a shelter in the cellars of the Empire Theatre but this was later felt to be unsuitable and it was agreed that the school would receive its own shelter. For this to be dug, however, part of the schoolyard, which was built over part of an old graveyard, would need to be dug up. Obviously, this would necessitate the removal of the remains and it was agreed that this work would only be carried out when the children were absent. One morning, however, the headmaster was aghast to find that some of the children had crawled under the tarpaulins used to cover the grave sites and were playing with several skulls.

Each separate community also had to have a control centre or headquarters which would act both as control and information processing centre in the event of raiding. In Stockton, the local council commandeered the ground floor of a disused engine works (Blair's) on Norton Road and set that up as its ARP headquarters. The borough was then divided into a number of sectors and a Councillor was placed as head warden in each sector. Problems faced by the head wardens included the ability to get around their assigned area. In Stockton's central sector a local butcher, Councillor Stoddart, was appointed as head warden and he put his Hillman 10 car at the disposal of the council, handily being granted extra petrol rations because of his position. Before the war, Councillor Stoddart toured the area in his car, distributing gas masks to the populace.

The warden service in Stockton appears to have been quite well organised from the off. Individual air raid wardens even had brass tiles fitted to the doors of their places of residence with air raid warden engraved upon them. This small idea helped because in the event of an alert off-duty wardens could quickly be brought to a state of alertness.

The warden service set up a series of posts in which wardens could be based and from which they went on patrol and called in incidents to HQ. In central Stockton, for example, posts were established at Mill Lane School (in the boilerhouse), Brunswick Methodist Church, and in the cellar of a tailor's shop in Mill Street West. The posts were manned twenty-four hours a day and each post had a number of messengers assigned to it in the event of an alert. These messengers were often Boy Scouts and other youths who were equipped with bicycles.

At this early stage of the war, when bombs had yet to be dropped on Britain, the wardens faced a great deal of resentment from a substantial proportion of the population. Wardens patrolling the streets, telling people to fix their blackout, to close doors or windows and other instructions tended to be seen as busybodies and this provoked feelings of resentment and animosity.

In Middlesbrough the ARP authorities set up their initial control centre in a disused church (the Unitarian Trinity Church) in Corporation Road and from here they oversaw the construction and placement of the necessary infrastructure for provision of ARP in the town. This included the erection of large static water tanks for firefighting, the placement of smaller water butts and sand barrels on many street corners, and a variety of other developments.

The rescue service in Middlesbrough had began in 1938 with eighty-four men being seconded from the Borough Engineer's Department of the council. The men were bricklayers, plumbers, joiners, painters, all experienced in manual work. They attended training lectures every week and officers were chosen by merit from those that had performed best in the compulsory exams.

As the realities of war hit home, however, it dawned on the authorities that many of these men were needed elsewhere and thus the rescue service was reorganised, with men from private building firms being recruited instead. These 'regulars' were backed up by hundreds of volunteers who were given rudimentary training. These men were recruited from among those who were experienced in heavy manual work, such as steelworkers or dockers. The regulars worked on a basis of twenty-four hours on and twenty-four hours off, and were supported by the volunteers who worked one shift a week which ran from 7 pm to 7 am. The men were organised into ten-strong squads bolstered by a squad leader. Two squads and a station officer were on duty at all times at every depot. The reorganisation resulted in a larger workforce, but training had suffered. To remedy this, each man was required to spend two fortnight-long spells at a training centre at Great Ayton.

Transport was again an issue and in the first months of the war the rescue squads were forced to use whatever vehicles were available or could be requisitioned, and a variety of hastily converted lorries formed the mainstay.

The duties of each particular squad at a depot depended largely upon which rota they were working that week. The first squad would inevitably be involved in incidents during a raid with the second squad then following up, often the next morning, to dig through the debris in a desperate search for survivors or, often, to recover bodies.

One of the key planks in the national plan to avoid unnecessary casualties in the event of war was the evacuations scheme. This would see children, very young children and their mothers, the disabled, some of the elderly and other vulnerable categories, evacuated from areas which were expected to come under attack. Much of the Middlesbrough area fell firmly into this category. Given the presence of so many important industries in the area (particularly iron and steel, chemicals, shipbuilding, and engineering) it was expected that the area would be a prime target for enemy bombing. The evacuation, nationally, began on 31 August, but in Middlesbrough the exodus from the town began on 8 September. Once again, the burden of organising the scheme at a local level fell upon an already stretched local authority.

This inevitably led to some confusion and some errors of judgement. One such perplexing error was that while pupils from Middlesbrough High School and Kirby Secondary School often lived next to one another in the same neighbourhoods, only the High School was initially included on the evacuation plan.

In the months leading to the war parents had been asked to consider putting the names of their children forward for the evacuation scheme and many thousands had done so. Rehearsal drills had also been held by many schools, with parents informed as to what their children should need on the day of evacuation. Arrangements had also been made with the areas in which children (and accompanying adults) would be billeted. In the case of Middlesbrough this, at first, included areas in rural parts of the North Riding of Yorkshire and the south-west of Co. Durham.

A large number of those who were evacuated found themselves in the seaside resort of Scarborough. This was another reflection of some of the muddle of the time as they should certainly not have been billeted in what was a vulnerable area of the east coast! The evacuees who found themselves billeted in the hotels and guest houses of Scarborough, however, were relatively fortunate. Food supplies, admittedly, were rather spartan and some of the residents of the town were not altogether pleased with the youthful inundation. One of the biggest problems was schooling. Parents back in Middlesbrough had been warned that children who remained in the town would receive no education as schools were to be closed (many being used by the authorities for other purposes), and those who were evacuated to Scarborough would receive very limited schooling as the local schools struggled to cope with the additional numbers. For the first weeks of their residence in the seaside town many of the evacuees had no formal schooling and spent the time enjoying themselves in the late summer. The bathing pools and the beach both proved very popular with the incomers, but gradually things became more organised.

With its strong maritime links, it is no surprise that a great many men from the area served in either the Royal Navy or the Merchant Navy.

A great many men were pre-war regulars in the Royal Navy and some found themselves in the early casualty lists as the Royal Navy suffered a number of severe misfortunes and reverses.

The Admiralty was well-aware of the threat presented from submarine warfare. After all, Britain had been nearly knocked out of the First World War by unrestricted submarine warfare. Convoy systems were already in place for many, but not all, merchant vessels but the military responses to the threat of the U-Boat menace were rather more problematic. In the first month of the war the Admiralty used fast aircraft carriers escorted by destroyers, organised into hunter-killer groups, to patrol likely areas but this was to prove disastrous and provided Orkney with its first fatalities of the war. On 14 September the aircraft carrier HMS *Ark Royal* was unsuccessfully attacked by a U-Boat, but lessons were not immediately learned and just three days later the converted aircraft carrier HMS *Courageous* was leading its own hunter-killer group in the Western Approaches.[1] During the evening of 17 September she was patrolling off the coast of Ireland when she was called to the assistance of a British merchant vessel which had been attacked. All of *Courageous'* aircraft had landed and she was preparing to launch a fresh wave when she was struck by two torpedoes fired from *U-29*. All electrical power was immediately lost, and the carrier capsized and sank within twenty minutes of being struck; 519 of her crew were lost.

Among the victims were two 21-year-old sailors from South Bank who had been close friends both before and after joining the Royal Navy. Stoker James Cooper, from 61 Middle Princess Street, had been in the RN for three years and had transferred to the *Courageous* less than three months earlier from HMS *Foresight*. His friend, Stoker Anthony Escritt of Lower Milbank Street, had joined the RN six months before his friend and had served aboard the *Courageous* for several months longer. Stoker Escritt's parents, Bob and Agnes, placed a notice in the press informing friends and family that a requiem mass was to be held at St Peter's Church, South Bank, on 23 September as well as thanking

*Stokers J. Cooper (l)
and A. Escritt (r).*
(North Eastern Gazette)

people, including the British Legion, for the condolences, letters and floral tributes which had been sent.

Another local man who had been aboard the stricken carrier found his experiences published in the local press. James Canfield was a naval veteran of eight years and a well-known musician in his home at Great Ayton. The 24-year-old had written home to his parents at Grange Mill telling how he had been joking with a friend who had recently been married when the first explosion occurred. Standing underneath an oil tank he had been drenched in oil which made him feel sick but which 'probably helped me to keep afloat', and which insulated him against some of the cold. He made for the deck where his first thought was that the carrier had hit a mine but, shortly afterwards, he saw the U-Boat which had targeted the *Courageous*. Almost immediately the order came to abandon ship and he threw himself into the sea. Canfield was in the sea for around an hour before a badly damaged boat from the carrier picked him up. The men in the boat struggled to keep it afloat, but after around twenty minutes they were picked up by a merchant ship. Showing typical Yorkshire humour he finished by commenting that he had suffered only cuts and bruises, but had lost all his possessions apart from his money which 'Being a good Yorkshireman I took good care to save.'[2]

The main anchorage for the Home Fleet was at Scapa Flow at Orkney. In mid-October, many of the fleet's ships were at sea or dispersed to other ports to provide security. The only battleworthy ship left at Scapa in the early hours of 14 October was the HMS *Royal Oak*, a First World War era battleship whose crew-list included a large number of boys under the age of 18. The only other large vessel present that night was the ageing seaplane carrier HMS *Pegasus*, which was anchored several miles away and invisible in the darkness of the early hours. Shortly after 1 am a small explosion was heard by some of the crew of *Royal Oak* and the anchor chain ran out. Most believed that an explosion of some sort had occurred in the forward inflammable store and, other than a check on magazine temperatures, most of those who had been awakened returned to their quarters. Skipper John Gatt of the drifter *Daisy II*, which had been lying alongside the battleship, heard the explosion and conferred with the officer of the watch aboard *Royal Oak*. Noticing that there was straw and wooden staves floating on the water alongside and knowing that this was usually used as packing for ships' stores, and that stores had been brought aboard *Royal Oak* the day before, he assumed that a minor internal explosion had occurred.

Approximately ten minutes later there were three larger explosions which caused a loss of electric power as well as destroying the Boys', Stokers' and Marines' messes, and an unexplained fireball swept through part of the ship from a secondary explosion. The ageing battleship quickly listed to starboard and water flooded in through open portholes and caused a far more serious list to develop. Less than ten minutes after the second set of explosions the battleship sank. Some men were able to scramble into a boat, others managed to clamber aboard the drifter *Daisy II* which had been lying alongside *Royal Oak*, while others found themselves in the water. The majority, however, remained trapped aboard the battleship as she went down.

For those in the water this was the beginning of a nightmare which took many more lives. The night was very dark, no lights were showing and the surface of the icy water was quickly covered in oil. Some, choking and gasping, struggled to the rocky shoreline nearby only to succumb to exposure or to be killed as they attempted to scale the cliffs in darkness.

The Middlesbrough and Teesside area suffered heavily in the tragedy and at least six sailors from the area lost their lives aboard the *Royal Oak*. One of the dead was a boy-sailor aged just 17. Boy 1st Class Leonard Frederick Willard was the youngest of four brothers and had joined the Royal Navy aged 16. He had written to his parents, George Henry and Martha Ann Willard, at their home at 28 Short Street, Middlesbrough, on a regular basis ever since. Len had served aboard HMS *Caledonia* before being posted to the *Royal Oak*. A keen and able lad he had been made leading boy and was training as a gunner. His love for the Royal Navy shone through in his final tragic missive, which was a postcard written just days before his death. In it, Len advised his parents to tell his 15-year-old cousin, Jackie Brown, 'to join the Navy if the war is still on when he is old enough. It is best even in wartime.' Len had been home on leave in July and had been looking forward to a forthcoming weekend leave. A week after Len's death his parents placed a message of thanks in the local newspaper in which they expressed their gratitude to relatives, friends and former teachers from St John's School. A memorial service for Len was held at the Seaman's Church on 29 October.[3]

When the war was approaching, many men from the Middlesbrough area were desperate to get into one of the services. Neil Blenkiron was one of these and, despite the fact that he had been involved with the Auxiliary Air Force before the war and was keen on flying, he had joined the Royal Navy in 1938. He was a time-served engineer, having previously been employed at Ridley Shaw & Co. at North Ormesby. On the morning of the day that the *Royal Oak* was sunk his parents (his father was a well-known figure in Middlesbrough and was employed by C. Garnett & Sons, Ltd, mineral water manufacturers) received a letter from him at their home at Westbourne Terrace in North Ormesby. In what was tragically to be his final letter, the 22-year-old Engine Room

Artificer 4th Class described his work in a cheerful style and spoke enthusiastically of his forthcoming engagement to Miss Mary Tighe, the daughter of the landlady of the Crown and Mitre Hotel.[4]

At Addesley Street in Stockton William and Alice Heslop received the news that their 18-year-old son, OS Cuthbert Heslop, had been one of those lost aboard the aged ship. OS Heslop had joined the Royal Navy aged just 17½, fulfilling a lifelong ambition, and had been immediately assigned to the *Royal Oak* following his training; he had served aboard the battleship for six months.[5]

Another victim who had been in the Royal Navy for just over a year was OS Thomas William Trenholm (20). The young sailor lived with his parents on Harehills Road, Acklam, had been a former pupil at Denmark Street School and had been a member of the Ward's Mission Boy's Brigade before the war.[6]

The body of Chief Stoker Jonah Williams was recovered after the sinking and the 38-year-old married man was buried at Lyness Royal Naval Cemetery. Chief Stoker Williams left behind his parents and

Above left: *Boy 1st Class Len Willard.* (North Eastern Gazette)

Above middle: *OS Cuthbert Heslop.* (North Eastern Gazette)

Above right: *Engine Room Artificer 4th Class Neil Blenkiron.* (North Eastern Gazette)

his wife, Isabel, at South Bank. Leading Stoker Henry Sidney Huggins was a married, 28-year-old, experienced sailor who left behind his wife, Helen Beatrice, and his parents, Frederick and May, in Middlesbrough.

November saw the Smith's Dock Co. Ltd. launch the 1,913-ton steam merchant *Norman Prince* (so named because it was the 1,066th ship produced by the firm) for Liverpool based Furness, Withy & Co. Ltd. before turning much of its production over to Admiralty contracts.

OS Thomas Trenholm. (North Eastern Gazette)

Although many people in Middlesbrough were left perplexed by the initial lack of decisive action during the first year of the war, one group who were fully aware that the war was being fought for real were the men of the Merchant Navy and their families. The merchant seamen were constantly at risk from enemy action in the form of U-Boats, surface craft, aircraft and mines, from the weather and even from collision (especially at night as they ran without lighting). On 3 December the Middlesbrough-registered SS *Moortoft* left Goole bound for Calais but nothing further was heard from the 879-ton merchantman. At least three Middlesbrough men lost their lives in the loss of the *Moortoft*. Demonstrating the cultural variety that the popularity of service in the Merchant Navy brought to the Middlesbrough area was the fact that two of the men were of Japanese extraction. Donkeyman S. Ito was a 51-year-old who left behind his wife, Margaret, in Middlesbrough, while Fireman Juiro Shimada was aged 48 and left behind his wife Rose Ann. The final Middlesbrough casualty on the *Moortoft* was another Fireman, Albert M. Diggnum, aged 46, another married man who left behind a widow, Elizabeth Gertrude Diggnum.[7] No trace of the *Moortoft* was ever found and it is believed that the ship foundered at sea.

CHAPTER 2

1940 – A Year of Trials

The first month of the year saw the widely anticipated introduction of food rationing and the people of Middlesbrough became slowly accustomed to the new routines of ration books, coupons and queues. The rationing system had meant a great deal of extra administrative work, with shoppers having to register with individual shops for specific rationed commodities. At first the weekly ration for an adult included just under a pound of sugar and two ounces each of bacon and butter. As the year progressed other items were added to the rationed list and amounts were altered as supplies were impacted by the ongoing war, loss of foreign markets and the Germans' use of submarine warfare. Items which appeared on the rationed list included sweets alongside staples such as eggs, cheese and tea, while margarine consumption increased even as the commodity was itself rationed.

The imposition of rationing was yet another factor in making people realise that the war was indeed real. Another sign on Teesside was the increasing levels of employment and the greater productivity of many of the traditional heavy industries. While the final touches were being made to the SS *Norman Prince* in 1939, the Smith's Dock company was working on the plans and construction of a prototype corvette for the Admiralty. The vessel was based on the design of a manoeuvrable whalecatcher built by the firm in 1936, and became the first of the 294 Flower-class corvettes to be built and serve during the war. It took the workforce just over five months to complete work on HMS *Gladiolus* and she was launched on 24 January.

The Flower-class went on to be a vital part of the Battle of the Atlantic as well as serving in numerous other theatres. There were, however, substantial teething problems with the type. Being based upon a mainly merchant vessel meant that the type had an unusual (for a warship) merchant-type bridge and a short forecastle. There were frequent complaints that crew quarters were poor and long-term habitability suffered as a result. It had been envisioned that the class would primarily serve around the coast and in the North Sea, but the needs of protecting convoys on the Atlantic meant that the first types, including *Gladiolus*, were immediately sent to serve in the Western Approaches. The heavier swells here badly affected the stability of the light and manoeuvrable corvettes. As a result of all these issues, many of the early models were recalled to be refitted with a longer forecastle and various other modifications, including ballast to increase stability. HMS *Gladiolus* herself was refitted in October 1940.

The problems experienced by the class were raised in parliament by the Conservative MP for Cleveland. Robert Tatton Bower, MP, had particular cause for raising the issue as he had been recalled as a serving commander in the RN and was appointed to take over command of a Flower-class corvette at South Bank. He had particular experience of the living conditions as his height had meant that alterations had to be made to his cabin before he could occupy it.[1]

As the year opened the Luftwaffe continued to score with attacks made on lone unescorted vessels. The tactics the Luftwaffe used usually involved two aircraft operating when there was cloud cover. Although press reports stated that while the efforts might gain some successes, the Luftwaffe were paying a very heavy price and had 'lost a quarter of their attacking numbers', the realities were that the Royal Navy and the Merchant Navy were paying a heavy toll in ships lost to these attacks.[2]

While the majority of workers were happy to tow the line given the national situation, there were others who were still willing to take illegal strike action to highlight their grievances. On 4 January, some 250 cutters and choppers working at the tailoring firm of Prices Ltd on Saltwells Road had walked out. The strike lasted just four days and the men agreed to go back to work under the condition that they could raise their grievances with the managing director, Mr I. Shuttleworth, when he visited Middlesbrough the following day.

The striking men had found little support either locally or nationally. Tailoring was seen as important due to the massive demand for items such as new battledress uniforms and other equipment, and strike action was viewed by many as being deeply unpatriotic. Those who had workplace grievances could no longer rely on their traditional forms of support from the unions as they had come to an agreement with the government which resulted in many unions not only discouraging men from taking industrial action, but actively briefing against them in the press.

With men and women working increased hours and with wartime restrictions already beginning to have an impact, it was seen as important that working folk had some opportunity for the release of tension through enjoyable pastimes. At this stage of the war attending a sporting match was still a possibility, although crowd sizes had been restricted. On 8 January, for example, 2,000 spectators saw Middlesbrough FC triumph 3-0 over Bradford City at Ayresome Park. By all accounts it was an entertaining match with Bradford having plenty of opportunities but failing to score, while Middlesbrough's front three of Fenton, Mannion and Murphy were particularly impressive. The first goal came after just three minutes when Murphy scored, but it was to be ten minutes into the second half before a second goal arrived with Wilf Mannion scoring a fine goal following a trademark dribble. The final goal came from Chadwick and the Middlesbrough supporters went home happy.

The iron and steel works which were present in Middlesbrough and its hinterlands were some of the area's leading and most important employers. With the advent of war they had become of critical importance to the national war effort. The works had taken on extra manpower in order to maintain the punishing wartime work schedules and to cope with the vastly increased demand for their products, and by the beginning of 1940 there were thousands of men employed.

The work for the majority of those employed in the iron and steel industries was of a very heavy manual type and many felt that the rations were somewhat meagre, considering the energy which workers in this industry expended. In December 1939, Middlesbrough Food Committee had made representations to ask about the possibility of increased rations for men employed in this vital area of industry. The committee had approached the Divisional Food Controller at Newcastle, Mr Angus Watson, to enquire about the possibility of an increased ration for those involved in manual work in heavy industry. Mr Watson expressed sympathy with their cause (he had also had deputations from several other local groups in the North East), but told them he would have to refer the matter to a national level. In January 1940, however, Mr Watson informed the Middlesbrough Food Control Committee that the Minister of Food had turned down the request, and a further blow came when he informed them that the Trades Union Congress (TUC) had agreed with the Minister. Mr Watson did, however, offer some hope telling the committee that if it could later be shown that real hardship was resulting from the rations, then the matter could be reappraised.

One of the largest and most famous companies was Dorman, Long & Co. Ltd. A firm of bridge builders and iron and steel manufacturers, the company had many wartime contracts. The work in the steel industry was dangerous as well as hard, and this was highlighted at the end of January when three of its workers were killed in an industrial accident. The incident happened at the company's rolling mills at Ayton. The three men, foreman Thomas Pain (58), Ernest Massey (37), and George Punshon (32) were clearing the main drain leading from the galvanising plant. One of the men entered the manhole which covered the entrance to the culvert but failed to return. A second man went in to investigate but also failed to return and Mr Pain, growing anxious, then entered also. When it was found that all three of the men had disappeared, an extensive search was carried out and the bodies of all three were discovered lying in a heap 8ft down, directly below the manhole.

An inquest came to the conclusion that the men had been overcome by fumes; the second two while attempting a rescue of their mates.

As we have already seen, the people of the Middlesbrough area had strong connections with the Royal Navy and news of ships that had been attacked brought consternation for many and anxiety for those who had loved ones serving. On 21 January the E-Class destroyer flotilla leader HMS *Exmouth* was escorting the merchant ship *Cyprian Prince* when she was torpedoed and sunk while still in the Moray Firth. The master of the merchantman deemed it too dangerous to stop to search for survivors after his vessel was fired upon and the destroyer went down with all 175 hands.[3]

Among the Middlesbrough dead from HMS *Exmouth* was AS Thomas William Lowery, a 43-year-old with twenty-four years' experience in the Royal Navy and a veteran of the Battle of Jutland in the First World War. Having left the RN, AS Lowery was on the reserve list and had been called up shortly before the start of the war. Lowery had been married for less than two years and it was his wife Mary who received the dreaded telegram at their home at 78 Granville Road. Mrs Lowery had been looking forward to seeing her husband as he was due home on leave on 27 January. AS Lowery's parents also lived in Middlesbrough and had been hoping that their son would be present at their golden wedding anniversary which was to be celebrated at Easter.[4] At least one more Middlesbrough veteran of the First World War also lost his life aboard HMS *Exmouth*. AS Guy Evans Morgan was a year older than his comrade AS Lowery and lived at Brecon Croft, Acklam Road, Linthorpe, Middlesbrough, with his parents, John Herbert and Marianne Morgan; it is highly likely that the two men knew one another.

The news of the recent naval losses resulted in the Mayor of Middlesbrough, Sir William Crosthwaite, agreeing to read the lesson at a special memorial service for the local men lost with HMS *Exmouth* and the merchant ships *Eston* and *Stanburn*. The service took place at the Middlesbrough Mission to Seamen on Sunday, 11 February,

Right: *AS Thomas William Lowery (seen as a young sailor in the First World War).* (North Eastern Gazette)

Below: *HMS* Exmouth. (North Eastern Gazette)

conducted by the Rev. J.R. Precious and held at the request of the National Union of Seamen and the Shipping Federation. Sir William asked as many people as possible to turn up and a large number were expected, so many that it was arranged that the service be relayed into the recreation room which lay below the church. Sir William had an intimate connection with mariners as he was owner of the Tees Towing Co. Ltd, a tug company.[5]

The SS *Eston* had sailed from Hull on the night of 26 January for the short journey to Blyth in Northumberland. Two days later she was reported to be lying off Blyth. The next morning she had vanished and nothing further was heard from the ship. Several days later the body of one of her seventeen crew was found in a lifeboat after it washed ashore on Tyneside. It was later established that the 1,487-ton steamer owned by P&O, which had been built in 1919, had sunk just 2,000 metres off Whitley Bay. Among the dead was Donkeyman George Liddle (63), a married man from Middlesbrough.[6]

The SS *Stanburn* was south-east of Flamborough Head on the day following the loss of the *Eston*, when several enemy dive bombers emerged from cloud cover and attacked. The *Stanburn* was struck by three bombs and sunk, taking with her the Master and twenty-five of her crew; there were only three survivors. At least two Middlesbrough men died aboard the SS *Stanburn*. Cook James Pirnie Goddard was a 48-year-old married man from Grove Hill, while Mess Room Boy Thomas Henry Mowbray was aged just 18 and was also from Grove Hill, living at 15 Bishopton Road. The body of Mr Mowbray was one of nine which were washed up on the Filey coast at the start of February.[7]

The Merchant Navy casualties continued for Middlesbrough when the SS *Leo Dawson* (formerly the SS *Roseden*) was lost while some fifteen miles east of the Shetlands on 2 February. The 4,330 ton merchantman had been missed by a torpedo at 9.11 pm, but a second torpedo hit and sunk her some fourteen minutes later. All thirty-five of her crew were lost. The crew included two very young Middlesbrough lads. OS Dominic Biesi was 18 and part of Middlesbrough's Italian community. OS Biesi left behind his parents, Mario and Maria Biesi in his hometown. Mess Room Boy John Wynn was aged just 15 and lived with his parents, Patrick Joseph and Mary Elizabeth Wynn.[8]

Two of Middlesbrough's twin merchant officers made headlines in early February when they achieved the feat of being introduced to the King and Queen. Back in September 1939 Master William Trowsdale's ship, the *Inverliffey*, had been sunk by a U-Boat and just a week later the King and Queen had been taken on a tour of his twin brother George's ship, the *Dunsley*, while it was docked at Victoria Docks in London. George had been so shocked after hearing of the loss of his brother's ship that he neglected to tell Their Majesties of it. On 8 February 1940 the King and Queen were introduced to William at Bristol. The twins had been inseparable companions and had attended school together before joining the Merchant Navy at the same time. The pair, aged 45, came from a seafaring family from Whitby (where George still lived) but both their parents and William (who was a bachelor) had moved to Middlesbrough before the war and lived at Heather Lea on Marton Road. When a reporter from the *North Eastern Gazette* called at their home to ask their reactions it came as a surprise to both parents as they had not yet heard of William being presented to Their Majesties. They were both thrilled to hear the news, especially Mr Trowsdale who was himself a former Master and had served more than forty years at sea with the Whitby firm of the Harrowing Steamship Co. The Trowsdale twins were two of five sons and the others were all involved in the maritime trade; one as London Trinity House pilot (who also held his captain's certificate), one worked in the office of the Constantine Shipping Company in Middlesbrough and one was employed as an engineer.

In order to help the local authorities and the police to enforce the blackout more effectively the RAF overflew many towns and cities in the North East in order to assess just how effective the blackout was in specific locations. The results of such a flight over Middlesbrough had shown that a great many motor-vehicles were not adequately shielding their head- or side-lamps. As a result of this the chief constable, Mr A.E. Edwards, asked all motorists to check their lights to ensure that they were conforming with the regulations. The chief constable also sent out a 'code of ethics' to all motorists in the area which gave instructions to them. He also invited them to call in at local police stations to have their lights checked and to receive advice if necessary. On the first

Master William Trowsdale.
(North Eastern Gazette)

Master George Trowsdale.
(North Eastern Gazette)

evening of the scheme some seventy or so motorists presented themselves and their vehicles for inspection.

As the Phoney War (or Bore War as it was known in Britain at the time) dragged on, the people of Middlesbrough and the surrounding area did their best to continue to raise funds for the war effort. Organisations and clubs of all stripes held dances and various other diversions to raise funds. Typical of these was the dance and whist drive which was held at Newman's Café, Stockton, in February by the men and women of the Stockton, Thornaby and District Grocers' Association. By these means the people of the area felt that they too were making an active contribution to the war. Many of the fundraising attempts at this stage of the war were to raise money for the Red Cross or to buy comforts for those serving in the forces.

With the need for entertainment key to the upkeep of morale on wartime Teesside, musical acts were always popular. In February the famed cinema and theatrical organist Reginald Foort was playing in Middlesbrough. Mr Foort had been named as the most popular radio entertainer in Britain in 1937 and was famous for his signature tune, 'Keep Smiling'. The musician had thrown himself into a punishing touring schedule during the war but ran into a series of misfortunes in Middlesbrough, culminating in a fire. Before the war Mr Foord had utilised six 6-ton vehicles to move his 25-ton organ while touring, but petrol rationing had meant this had been cut down to two vehicles while the rest of the organ was transported by train. In the early hours of 9 February, a patrolling policeman noticed flames coming from the roof of the North Ormesby Road garage premises of Messrs James Smith (Transporters) Ltd. The garage was being used to house one of Mr Foort's transports along with a mobile recording unit. By the

Above left: *Stockton, Thornaby and District Grocers' Association.* (North Eastern Gazette)

Above right: *Reginald Foort.* (Public Domain)

time the fire brigade arrived both vehicles were well alight and the fire brigade could not prevent their destruction. Fortunately, Mr Foort's other transporter and a vehicle carrying valuable electrical equipment were being housed in a nearby outhouse and were not affected. The greatest monetary loss was the recording unit, which was the most advanced of its kind in the world and worth at least £10,000, while the transporter held sentimental value having been with Mr Foort throughout his career. Despite admitting that the loss was 'a bitter blow' he said he would continue following his motto and 'keep smiling'.[9]

By March the rationed goods list had expanded to include meat, which was rationed by price. Butchers therefore became figures of quiet influence in many Middlesbrough communities as housewives depended upon them to secure a meat supply for the family. Although prime and cheap cuts were rationed, some items remained off the list and thus found new popularity. Sausages were always popular, but the ever-decreasing meat content in the wartime sausage was a constant source of complaint, as were pies (which attracted the same complaints as did sausages) and poultry, but so too did various forms of offal.

One of the most common aspects of wartime life in Middlesbrough which was a direct result of rationing and food shortages was the queue. It became an increasing part of the life of the average householder to have to get accustomed to queuing, sometimes for hours, to obtain items which in peacetime were readily available. Bread, fresh fruit and vegetables, fish and potatoes were not always available for purchase, and even when they were, often in short supply with many at the tail of queues being left disappointed. This was one reason why campaigns such as 'Dig for Victory' were so successful. People were increasingly willing to put in the effort to grow and produce their own food, and poultry and pig clubs were both popular and successful.

Many of the evacuees who had left Middlesbrough in September 1939 had returned home by the early months of 1940. Loneliness, homesickness, the wish to be together as a family regardless of the dangers, all played a role in the motives of returnees. Schools in the town gradually reopened (often on a shift basis with half pupils attending in the morning and the other half in the afternoon). Middlesbrough High School, for example, which had been partially reopened in 1939 was fully reopened by April 1940, with almost all of its pupils having returned.

On 25 March there was another wartime marriage ceremony involving a Middlesbrough serviceman. This one, though, attracted the attention of the media as it involved one of the first RAF heroes of the war. On 19 September 1939, Sgt William Edward Willits (25) had been the second pilot and navigator aboard an Avro Anson on 269 Squadron flying a patrol over the North Sea from its base at RAF Montrose. The Anson had encountered an enemy seaplane and a clash occurred during which the pilot of the British aircraft, P/O Dennis Samuel Martin Burrell, was shot through the head and killed. His body fell across the controls and as the aircraft was at low level, there was a great danger it would crash; Sgt Willits acted quickly and managed to get control so that the rest of the crew could pull P/O Burrell's body off the controls. Sgt Willits thereafter managed to pilot and navigate the aircraft the 140 miles back to base where he landed, saving the remaining crew. On 3 November 1939, Sgt Willits had been gazetted with the DFM, becoming the first airman of the war to be awarded this medal.[10] Sgt Willits, who lived at 71 Ayresome Street, was typically modest about his exploits and had not told anyone before the award of his medal. He was married at Pembroke Dock to Dorothy Brown, a telephonist at the Pembroke Dock Post Office. Sgt Willits had joined the RAF in 1936 and went on to have a very successful wartime career in the service.

The attitudes of many civilians in the area was that of boredom as the Phoney War dragged on, but others maintained an aggressively patriotic attitude. As the year opened the ARP services in the area continued to practice and to learn. In Stockton, for example, an exercise was held in which a bomb was supposed to have exploded in a crowded working-class area close to Garbutt Street. One of those responsible for refereeing the exercise in order to assess the effectiveness of the ARP services was the deputy head warden of central Stockton, Mr T. Sowler. The deputy head warden was standing in the street when an elderly woman came out of one of the houses to enquire what was going on. When explained to her, she vehemently told the warden that she would oppose any German who landed nearby. She then provided evidence of this by going into her outhouse and emerging with a piece of wood in which a large number of rusty nails had been driven (possibly it was a trench club left over from the First World War), and telling the warden that she intended to use the makeshift weapon to kill any German she came across.

The ARP services in the area were, however, gradually becoming more efficient. Some organisational lessons had been learned from other areas and training had become more effective, while the issues of equipment were helping to improve both effectiveness and morale. The rescue squads, for example, were able to replace many of their adapted lorries with especially built rescue and salvage vehicles while specialised tools for burrowing into piles of debris were also being issued. Clothing, too, had improved with the men now being able to wear heavy-duty denims when on duty, and issues of anti-gas clothing also became more frequent.

The perception that the war was an inactive one was shattered by the German invasions of Denmark and Norway, followed on 10 May by the invasion of France and the Low Countries. Suddenly, the war was real. This was the case for the people of Middlesbrough too as the town gained the dubious honour of becoming the first industrial area to be bombed by the enemy. The event occurred on 25 May, when five bombs exploded at Cargo Fleet followed by seven at South Bank and Grangetown. One bomb hit the roof of a building at Cargo Fleet Works while another fell in the grounds, but damage was limited. At Dorman Long's South Works eight men were injured with three of them requiring hospital treatment.

At Aire Street in South Bank a bomb caused extensive damage to a number of houses and outbuildings. Thankfully, no serious injuries occurred despite several residents reporting lucky escapes. These included a 10-year-old girl who was discovered still asleep on her bed – despite being covered in broken glass and splintered woodwork. The air raid sirens had not sounded to alert people to the impending danger and this fact caused a great deal of angry comment in the next few hours and days. Locals also complained that the anti-aircraft defence of the area did not fire upon the enemy aircraft, even though it had been heard circling the area for some time. One of the bombs dropped by the intruder had fallen on South Bank football ground and had landed almost exactly on one of the penalty spots, leaving behind a large crater but little structural damage to the stadium.

With the Phoney War over, one of the many concerns was, once again, the fate of children and the vulnerable in the event of bombing or invasion and there was another wave of evacuations. These were less successful in terms of numbers but many of those families who could, organised their own evacuation by renting a rural property in the hinterlands. In this second evacuation some lessons had been learned and the evacuees found themselves sent inland to areas such as Upper Teesdale. While these smaller communities were undoubtedly safer than the likes of Scarborough, there were other difficulties. The small villages and towns did not have the hotels and boarding houses of resorts and so children had to be split up and housed individually or in small numbers in private homes. Schooling was again a problem with the small village schools unable to cope adequately with the increase in numbers. In many cases this badly disrupted the education of children, while those who were luckier often found themselves being schooled in an unusual setting, such as Bowes Museum. Once again, however, for many the evacuation did not last. Although the bombing of Middlesbrough focused minds, the majority of families came to the conclusion that they would rather face the dangers together and children drifted back home in droves.

The situation in France looked increasingly dire, and if they were defeated, Britain faced the possibility of imminent invasion; as a result, the government gave in to demands for a citizen force to resist an invader, or at least to assist the regular forces in doing so. When men were asked to come forward to join a new force to be known as the Local Defence Volunteers (LDV), it was expected that a relatively small number would respond. The government completely underestimated the mood in the country and hundreds of thousands surged forward to put their names down in the days and weeks that followed.

Organisation of this new ad-hoc force was hopelessly complicated at first. In urban Teesside many men were working in reserved occupations in heavy industry and many of these companies, eager to be seen to be patriotic, helped workers form their own units which were gradually absorbed into the county structure. In the rural hinterlands it was different.

In the pretty and picturesque market town of Yarm the typical pattern was followed, with a retired army officer and well-known figure in local society taking charge. In this case it was Major Kenneth Evans of Worsall Hall who took charge of the Yarm LDV. Unlike their urban counterparts, the members of the Yarm LDV were a mixture largely of men who worked on farms and in the small villages and the market town itself. As with all LDV, the men at first did not even possess a uniform, merely an arm-band with the initials LDV printed upon it, and their status in the event of an invasion was uncertain, with the Germans threatening to shoot them as *Franc-tireurs*. Nevertheless, the men of the LDV set about their duties guarding vital structures such as railway lines and reservoirs with whatever weaponry could be begged or borrowed. Often this meant shotguns and even converted pikes using whatever farming tools were handy and available.

One consequence of the fall of France and the Dunkirk evacuation was that the remnants of the British Army were in no way equipped to face the possibility of a large-scale invasion. The vast majority of the BEF's heavier equipment and vehicles, as well as many lighter weapons, had been abandoned in France and Belgium and replacing them would take time. Manpower was also an issue and it would take time to recruit and train the young men who had volunteered. This meant that the LDV attracted new popularity and importance, as well as influence.

Attitudes towards the men of the LDV varied widely. While some acknowledged that the men were volunteering to help the war effort, often teaming this with a hard manual job, the majority were somewhat scornful of the rag-tag force which appeared to some to be merely middle-aged and older men playing at being soldiers and getting in the way as people went about their business.

As uniforms and then weapons arrived, however, the attitude to, and of, the LDV began to change. There was still much widespread resentment in the force at what they saw as an official attitude of despairing reluctance towards them. The widespread nickname of 'Look, Duck and Vanish' was hastily conferred by many and caused more resentment and ridicule. Ordered to undertake purely defensive, or even observational duties the men of the LDV rankled at this restraint and urged for a more active role. Others simply took this upon themselves and began making more militant plans of their own.

In Yarm the arrival of the first weaponry, consisting of old Canadian Ross rifles and hand grenades, was eagerly met, and a nearby warehouse in the town was hastily converted into a makeshift armoury in which guns, grenades and all manner of handmade devices were stored. By July the force had been renamed, at the insistence of Churchill, as the Home Guard, and in August a more aggressive role was envisioned and outlined. As the year progressed the Home Guard units of Teesside became better trained and better equipped. With these improvements came an increase in respect.

Certainly, the Home Guard proved their worth even at this early stage of the war by relieving regular soldiers of mundane guard tasks and other duties. Despite the growing level of ability and professionalism in many units there were still incidents which highlighted the firmly amateur nature of the Home Guard. At Yarm, one member remembered how they had been put on parade as a high-ranking officer from nearby Catterick was to pass through the town. The dignitary was late and the Home Guard lined up on the High Street were growing increasingly restive. Typically, for the heart of a Home Guard unit was often a public house, they repaired to the nearest pub, in this case the Black Bull. This meant that when the dignitary did arrive, he did not receive the welcome he had anticipated.

The same member remembered another occasion when the Yarm unit were on an exercise near Northallerton. They were to sneak up on a position and their route took them through an orchard at the rear of a pub. The unit took full advantage of the opportunity to empty the orchard of its apples.

Many of the weapons which found their way into the hands of the Home Guard were experimental in nature and the testing of them could often be problematic. The Yarm company were issued with one of the notoriously difficult to operate Blacker Bombard mortars, and set up to test the weapon by firing it with a blank shell. It was decided that the mortar would be fired across the river into the woods at Almond's Bottoms from a position in the gardens of the Friarage. A section of men had been sent to clear the target area and had reported it empty, so the shot was fired successfully. Upon landing, however, the blank round scared a couple who had been enjoying a romantic tryst in the woods and the Home Guards no doubt had a good laugh as the young couple fled in alarm.

The aerial bombing of England had begun on the night of 21/22 June when German aircraft dropped mines off the coast and carried out reconnaissance and limited bombing attacks across the North-East. Reports in Middlesbrough are very scant and there is little mention, other that an incident did take place. This resulted in the death of an air raid warden, Mr Isaac John James Cooper (27), of 222 Stockton Road, who died in North Riding Infirmary.

The importance of keeping even small ports open to shipping meant constant work. The work to do this was of a highly dangerous nature and the entrances to ports had to be constantly swept for mines. The minesweepers undertaking these duties suffered continuous losses, but so too did other vessels. On 4 July the bucket dredger SS *Coquetmouth* was working to keep the harbour of Amble in Northumberland open when she detonated a magnetic mine and immediately began to sink while just half a mile off the harbour entrance. Most of the crew were rescued but three men died. Among them was 66-year-old Deck Hand James Brown, a married man from Linthorpe.[11]

On 1 July HMS *Gladiolus* participated in the sinking of *U-26*, the first sinking of a submarine by a corvette. Just days earlier she had picked up thirty-five survivors from the SS *Llanarth* and when she picked up a contact the corvette immediately launched a depth charge attack. The *Gladiolus* dropped eight charges and was joined in the attack by an RAF Coastal Command Short Sunderland, which dropped several bombs. The *U-26* was badly damaged and forced to the surface before her crew scuttled her.

The long summer nights were at odds with the dark turn of events. On the night of 26 July the blackout began shortly before 10.15 pm, but only an hour later the alarms began to sound and people in Middlesbrough and the surrounding areas took to their shelters. Indeed, almost the entirety of the North-East was in a condition of alert for almost the entire night. In the early hours of 27 July a stick of bombs fell in a rough line between the Transporter Bridge and Middlesbrough Town Hall and did considerable damage, to the value of many thousands of pounds. The first bomb hit and badly damaged the Anderston Foundry close to the northern side of the Transporter Bridge, another narrowly missed the bridge itself but caused damage to the car and overhead cables. St Peter's Church and the neighbouring vicarage were both destroyed together with a warehouse and a nearby signal box. The vicar of St Peter's was on duty at the time as a warden and his wife and young daughter had an even more fortunate escape. They would ordinarily have been occupying the cellar of the destroyed vicarage but had gone on holiday just two days earlier. At Town Hall corner, the junction of Albert Road and Corporation Road, a bomb hit some public toilets which were erected under the clock tower and blew out windows across a wide area as well as causing structural damage.

On 22 July Mr T. Sowler, the deputy head warden for central Stockton who had been so bemused by the aggressive intentions of an elderly lady months earlier, was getting married at Holy Trinity Church. Even here, however, he was not immune from the war. In the midst of the ceremony a warden came into the church to inform the congregation that a yellow alert had been sounded. Fortunately, Mr Sowler kept his head and insisted the ceremony continue, aware of the fact that if the alert was upgraded to red and the sirens sounded he would have to leave to undertake his duties. Fortunately, this did not happen and the marriage was completed. The war continued to intrude, however, and the unfortunate Mr Sowler was recalled from his honeymoon to be asked to consider taking up a reserved occupation (he was a teacher) so that he would not be lost to the services. Mr Sowler refused and later joined the RAF.

The August holiday saw some school-age children give up their usual pursuits in order to make a more patriotic contribution to the war effort.

In Stockton, around twenty pupils and several masters from Stockton Grammar School volunteered to undertake forestry duties at a Forestry Commission plantation which was being harvested of thousands of tons of timber. The group were put up at a guest house a couple of miles from the plantation and got up at 7 am each morning to cycle or walk to work. Beginning at 9 am, they worked until lunchtime when they had a half-hour break for lunch. They then resumed work until finishing time at 3 pm. The group finished their month-long 'holiday' on 22 August and when they returned to Thornaby Station they were met by a reporter and a photographer from the local press who found the boys in good spirits. One boy described the experience as a 'glorious holiday' in which they had gone to bed very tired every night and with sore muscles, but told the reporter that they had soon grown accustomed to the hard work and had found it very rewarding.

All of the group insisted that they would gladly undertake another such holiday and Mr C. Goulding, the master-in-charge, said that the Forestry Commission policy of encouraging strong boys to give their services to the nation in such a way was a very sound one, benefiting the nation and the boys themselves. Mr Goulding told the reporter that the boys had gone about their work cheerfully and had done almost as much work as experienced men considering their pay of 6d per day for over-16s and 5d per day for those under 16.

Perhaps seeking to encourage more schools to join in and to reassure parents, Mr Goulding was at pains to say that the guest house in which the boys had been put up was comfortable and provided them with good beds and food. The lads had spent their evenings playing tennis and bowls or walking or cycling in the surrounding area. They had also been lucky with the weather, only experiencing rain on one day.

On 25/26 August the Luftwaffe returned to the North-East. On Teesside the bombing was fairly limited but resulted in four deaths. In Robert Street, Grangetown, two special constables were killed when their post was hit. Hulbert Whitworth Adams was a 63-year-old from 13 Argyle Road, while his colleague, Edwin Henry Brooks, was aged 46 and from 13 Granville Road. At 1 Railway Place, 9-year-old Mavis Hewett was badly injured and rushed to Eston Hospital where she died of her injuries. In Stockton, three or four bombs destroyed a shed and damaged three railway engines at the Tyne-Tees Wharf, while a small workshop making munitions and a store belonging to the Ministry of Food were also hit. Both high explosives and incendiaries fell on the Victoria Bridge between Stockton and Thornaby. Harold Cecil Ewles (44) was unlucky enough to be on the bridge at the time and was severely wounded; he died in hospital later that day. Mr Ewles was originally from Norwich but was married and lived at 55 Laurel Road. The shrapnel damage that was caused to the bridge can still be seen.

The Luftwaffe returned in small numbers over the next few nights. In the early hours of 28 August, a bomb at Port Clarence seriously injured two people and three others were less seriously hurt. No. 25 Meadowfield Avenue, Middlesbrough, was destroyed by a bomb during this raid and Lilian Morley, the 40-year-old wife of an air raid warden, who was carrying her 2-year-old baby down to the shelter, was killed. The child, along with two others who were downstairs survived. A further nineteen bombs fell in the neighbouring area and the numbers of those bombed out meant that a feeding centre at Marton Grove School had to be opened. Three wardens had a lucky escape when a bomb completely destroyed another house in Meadowfield Avenue. The three were sheltering in an alley next to the house but were unhurt, although badly shaken.

Even as the Battle of Britain raged at the end of August some Middlesbrough families were still awaiting news of loved ones that had been posted missing during the fall of France. For Sarah Hannah Rigg, the quest for information about her husband was to end in grief. Pvt Joseph Dobson Rigg of 76 Marshalls Avenue, Bramble Farm, had been serving with 2 DLI, but the 33-year-old was later confirmed as having been killed at some time between 23–31 May. His body was laid to rest in St Venant Communal Cemetery and his widow had the following inscription placed upon his headstone: 'HE SLEEPS IN GOD'S BEAUTIFUL GARDEN LOVINGLY REMEMBERED BY WIFE, DAUGHTERS AND SON'.

Others received better news and the end of August brought news that two Middlesbrough men and a soldier from Stockton had all been confirmed as having survived as PoWs. They were Fusilier F. Hatton of 26 Atkinson Street, Middlesbrough, Pvt E. Humphrey from 31 Stowe Street, Middlesbrough, and Pvt B. Jones of 16½ Farrer Street, Stockton.

Many families from the Middlesbrough area had particular cause for anxiety as they had several loved ones serving in France. These men were a mixture of regular soldiers and members of the Territorials whose battalions had been sent to France. A number of regiments that had substantial numbers of men from the area within their ranks were present in France, Belgium and Holland at the time of the German invasion.

Missing soldiers. Top to bottom (l-r): Fusilier F.Hatton, Pvt B. Jones, Pvt J.D. Rigg, and Pvt E. Humphrey. (North Eastern Gazette)

With the Royal Navy mounting desperate efforts to pull as many troops as possible off the beaches of Dunkirk, the losses to German aircraft continued to mount as attacks intensified. Ships and boats of almost every description were utilised in the evacuation. From the famed 'small ships', many of which were partially or wholly crewed by RN personnel, to destroyers and even larger vessels which stood offshore to pick up survivors. Smaller ships picked up troops from the beaches themselves. Among these vessels were minesweepers and trawlers which on a daily basis took phenomenal risks to rescue men. HMS *Skipjack* was one of the minesweepers which was involved in the evacuation. A Halcyon-class fleet minesweeper, *Skipjack* had been in dock at Grimsby for a five-week long refit, but set sail for Dover on 26 May. By 1 June she was off Dunkirk picking up troops. Under sustained and heavy air attack, the minesweeper circled in an evasion pattern only straightening to make repeated runs to the beach to pick up soldiers. By 8.44 am the minesweeper was packed with an estimated 275 soldiers aboard (the majority crammed below decks) and had run out of ammunition. As she attempted to make her way away from the area she was attacked by a large force of aircraft including Ju87 Stuka dive bombers and Ju88 bombers. *Skipjack* was hit and seemed to lose power and began to list to port, a sitting target she was then hit by a further three bombs and at 8.49 am she turned turtle and sank. Survivors who managed to escape the sinking craft found themselves being machine-gunned in the water by the attacking aircraft and nineteen of her crew and 275 troops were lost. Among the dead from the minesweeper was Stoker 1st Class William Graham Stephenson (37), a married sailor from Middlesbrough.[12]

For many families with loved ones in the services this period was one of acute anxiety as the chaos of the fall of France and the evacuation from Dunkirk meant that many records were lost and others took time to update and confirm. This meant that many families faced a wait to find out the fate of loved ones who had initially been posted as missing. The Wright family of 13 Alder Road, Stockton, had more reason than most to be anxious as they had five brothers in the Army. By the end of May two of the brothers had been posted as missing in action. Both men were serving with 2 Durham Light Infantry (DLI). Sgt Stanley Wright (26) was an eight-year veteran, while his younger brother Pvt Ronald Wright (21) had been in the Army for three years. Sgt Wright had been posted missing on 26 May, but it was September before it was confirmed that he had been wounded and was a PoW. After treatment for his wounds Sgt Wright was held at Stalag 357 at Oerbke and survived his captivity, being free by May 1945. His younger brother was not so fortunate and the agonising wait for their parents, John and Mary, went on until it became obvious that Ronald had lost his life. This news, however, was not officially confirmed until the end of March 1943. The remaining three brothers were Sgt Herbert Wright (31) who had served with the DLI but transferred to the Royal Northumberland Fusiliers (RNF), Pvt John William Wright (29) who was serving with a Territorial battalion of the King's Own Royal Rifles, and Pvt Arthur Wright (18) who was with the Green Howards.

A large proportion of those who had been reported missing during the period turned out to be alive and PoWs. A large number of these had been serving with the Territorials in 4 Green Howards.[13] On 19 June Mr and Mrs Chandler of 193 Union Street, Middlesbrough, received the news that their son, Pvt Thomas Chandler (22), had been posted missing. Pvt Chandler had been serving with 4 Green Howards and it was not until August that they received the news that he had been taken prisoner and was at Stalag 20a at Thorn Podgorz in Poland. On the same day that Pvt Chandler was declared missing, another Middlesbrough family received the news that their son had shared that fate. Pvt Thomas Henry (19) had joined the Territorials shortly before the outbreak of war and was serving in France with the same battalion as Pvt Chandler. Once again, the news was not as bad as it

Pvt Thomas Chandler (l)
and Pvt Thomas Henry (r).
(North Eastern Gazette)

could have been and Mr and Mrs Henry received word at their home at 49 Bruce Avenue, Acklam, that their son was a PoW at Stalag 20b at Marienburg.[14]

Like many, Pvt W. Hurst had joined up shortly before the start of the war only to become another member of the battalion to be taken prisoner in France. His wife in North Ormesby and his mother in Middlesbrough no doubt received the news with a mixture of relief and trepidation.

At 7 Wood Street, Stockton, the parents of twenty-year veteran Platoon Sergeant Major (PSM) George Pinkney were informed that their son too had been posted missing in action while serving with 2 DLI. The worry must have been particularly acute as PSM Pinkney had a wife and four young sons at his home in Torquay, but it was later confirmed that he had been taken as a PoW and was being held at Stalag 383 at Hohen Fels. The family must have reacted with some relief which would have been followed by pride when it was revealed that PSM Pinkney was to be awarded the Distinguished Conduct Medal (DCM), and this was duly gazetted on 20 December 1940. The full citation read:

On 15 May 1940, the German Army attacked the 2nd Battalion DLI across the River Dyle, east of Brussels. 'B' Company was pushed back and the Commanding Officer ordered 'C' Company to counter attack. One platoon was destroyed. The other led by Platoon Sergeant Major Pinkney, an old soldier who had enlisted in 1920, forced the Germans back across the river. On 27 May at Saint Venant, 2 DLI was overwhelmed by German armour. Sergeant Pinkney was last seen attacking the tanks with a box of grenades. He survived but spent the rest of the war as a prisoner. For his 'example and courage', George Pinkney was awarded the Distinguished Conduct Medal – one of the first awarded during the Second World War.

For another Stockton family the news was not so positive. Gnr George Askey was a 36-year-old married man who had been in the Army for seventeen years. At the time of the invasion of France he was serving with 228 Battery, 57 (1/5 East Surrey Regt) Anti-Tank Regt, Royal Artillery. His wife Winifred received news that he was missing at their home on Compton Street, but a few weeks later it was confirmed that he had been killed in action between 31 May and 2 June.[15]

The other Territorial battalion of the Green Howards, the 5th, was also in France. Corporal Robert Strickland was the son of a Pickering councillor and before the war he had worked at his father's firm as well as being secretary of the Pickering Toc H. A keen member of the Territorials he had been married to a Southgate woman on his last leave and it was his wife who received the news that he had been posted missing. It was later ascertained that he too had been taken prisoner and was incarcerated at Stalag 357.

At 118 Crescent Road, Middlesbrough, George and Annie Newton received news that their son, Pvt Arthur Newton (28), 6 Argyll & Sutherland Highlanders, had been posted missing in France. Like so many in that chaotic period no further news was ever received and the young soldier simply vanished. It was not until late May 1943 that he was confirmed as having been killed in action. Pvt Newton was another man who had joined up in 1939 when war appeared inevitable.[16]

Trooper Henry 'Harry' Orton was a 21-year-old native of Co. Durham, but in 1940 he was registered as living with his wife at 43 Mill Street, Middlesbrough. His parents also lived in the town, at 1 Baker Street and it was here that they received the telegram notifying them that their son had been posted missing in France while serving with 1st Fife and Forfar Yeomanry, Royal Armoured Corps. It was at the end of November 1941 that they received news that he had been confirmed as having been killed in action on 21 May 1940.[17]

A number of older men who had previously served in the Army and were still on the reserve list found themselves called up at the start of the war and many afterwards found themselves in France. Numbers of men who had served previously in the Army and were still on the reserve list were recalled at the outbreak of war and many were posted to France, among them was Pvt William Brogden. At the time he was recalled, to serve in the Royal Army Medical Corps (RAMC), he was living at 1 Wood Street, Middlesbrough. His mother, Mrs Alice Hey, received news of his being posted missing at her home at 1 Grimwood Avenue, Brambles Farm, before receiving confirmation weeks later that her son was a PoW. For unreported reasons, Pvt Brogden did not remain a prisoner as he was repatriated in November 1943. It is likely that he had suffered a serious wound or illness, or it may have been that he was simply judged to be too old to be a future combatant.

Given its importance as a port and its shipbuilding history it is no surprise that the activities of the Merchant Navy were a constant source of both interest and anxiety. The many Middlesbrough men who served in the Merchant Navy understood that during war their jobs were high risk. While those in the Royal Navy could fight back this was rarely an option for the men of the Merchant Navy.

Merchant vessels were unarmoured and not designed to provide cover for their crews against bombs, or cannon and machine-gun fire, so although a ship might not sink there were often casualties among the crew. In August, the storeship MV *Beal* had been attacked and her Master severely wounded. The *Beal* too had been at Dunkirk, where she had rescued some 364 men from the beaches. The Middlesbrough Master of the *Beal*, however, did not survive his injuries and died in North Ormesby Hospital on 19 August. His funeral in Middlesbrough attracted a large number of mourners, led by his widow Florence May Crackles and his daughter.[18]

On 24 August another Middlesbrough naval veteran of the First World War lost his life in this new conflict. Stoker Michael Byrne (42) had served throughout the first conflict and had been called up shortly before the outbreak of war in 1939. By August 1940 he was serving aboard the Hastings-class sloop HMS *Penzance*. The ship was in Canada but was ordered home, and on that journey was the sole armed escort to Convoy SC-1. On 24 August she was some 700 miles south-west of Iceland when a torpedo struck her starboard flank.

The MV Beal *(here seen after the war as the* Sylvian Coast*)*. (Unknown)

The sloop broke in half, with some of her depth charges exploding, and sank very quickly with the loss of 90 of her 104 crew, including Stoker Byrne. His widow, Margaret Ellen, received news of his death at their home at 109 Glebe Road. She had previously been notified that he had been posted missing but initially there appears to have been some hope that he had been rescued; sadly, his death was confirmed in November 1940. Stoker Byrne left behind not only his wife, but also three daughters (Marie, Jean and Vera) and three unnamed stepsons.[19]

As the Battle of Britain occupied the minds of much of the country there were those in Middlesbrough who followed events in the air particularly keenly as they had loved ones serving in the RAF. Flight Lieutenant William Edward Gore, DFC, had been born in Middlesbrough. After an education at Red House School and the gaining of a BSc at Durham University he had gained a research position with the Hebburn-on-Tyne firm of Reyrolle. A keen member of 607 (County Durham) Squadron of the Auxiliary Air Force the Battle of Britain found him as a 25-year-old section leader. On 31 May he was awarded the DFC for an action in which he and his section had shot down three German bombers over France. On 28 September, however, he was shot down and killed during an encounter with Messerschmidt

HMS Penzance. (Public Domain)

Bf109 fighters over the Channel. His body was never recovered and he is commemorated on the Runnymede Memorial. In 1943 his younger brother, Lieutenant John Lionel Gore was killed in north Africa while serving with the West Yorkshire Regiment.

It was not only the men of RAF Fighter Command who were taking part in the Battle of Britain. Those of Army Cooperation, Bomber, and Coastal Commands were all involved and all suffered casualties. On what was to be recorded as the second night of the Battle of Britain Bomber Command sent aircraft to bomb several targets. Sgt Charles Suggett was an air gunner with 149 Squadron but he and his crew failed to return from an operation to Bremen on this night.

In the early hours of 12 August Wellington IC (P9244, OJ-E) of 149 Squadron was returning to its base at RAF Mildenhall following a raid on Gelsenkirchen. At 3:48 am the Wellington was making an approach but was wide of the flare path (it seems that the Wellington may have been experiencing problems with its undercarriage) when it struck a radio mast and crashed, killing all who were on the aircraft. The second pilot in the crew was a Middlesbrough man, Pilot Officer John Body. Tragically, P/O Body's brother P/O Stephen Body was killed in a flying accident less than a month later when his Miles Master of 7 Operational Training Unit (OTU) crashed on 9 September.

The night following the loss of P/O John Body Bomber Command was once again active. The Hampdens of 61 Squadron, based at RAF Hemswell, were sent to Salzbergen. Two of the aircraft from the squadron failed to return. Amongst them was that of P/O H.C. Sheldon. The air gunner in the crew was yet another Middlesbrough airman. Sgt Charles Edward Thrower was buried alongside his crew at Hamburg Cemetery.

Many RAF squadrons that had taken part in the ill-fated Battle of France had returned battered and been reformed and re-equipped before re-entering the fray. The Fairey Battles of 105 Squadron had been decimated and upon its return to Britain the squadron had been re-equipped with the Bristol Blenheim and used in strikes against German held airfields and ports. On 1 September Middlesbrough observer Sgt Harry Horatio Duncan (23) was wounded while on one of these operations and he later died of his wounds.

On 30 September Lockheed Hudson T9326 of 224 Squadron took off from its base at Aldergrove, Co. Antrim, to carry out a lengthy anti-submarine patrol. Almost immediately after take off the Hudson lost all power and crashed with the loss of all five men aboard. Sgt John Patrick O'Connor was listed as a flight mechanic and was buried at North Ormesby.

On 7 October another Middlesbrough air gunner lost his life in a tragic accident. Sgt Marcus Rudolph Harvey (29) was an experienced airman and, as was fairly common, had been assigned to fly a coastal reconnaissance mission with a newly arrived pilot. After completing the reconnaissance the Lysander was ordered to return to base but instead flew to Carlton in Cleveland which was the site of a divisional headquarters with which 4 Squadron of Army Cooperation Command worked often. It would seem that the experienced air gunner was giving his pilot a tour of the local landmarks for his future benefit. The Lysander made several low passes over a message-dropping field but shortly before 8 am it was seen to dive at high speed into the ground from a height of 50 feet. It would seem that the pilot had become disorientated by the low level he was flying. Both crew were killed instantly.

Life on wartime Teesside could be grim, with the blackout, rationing and shortages, anxiety over loved ones, and the threat of air raids all playing a role in dampening morale. It was vital that the civilian population had some outlet for recreation and enjoyment and the most popular of all was the cinema. Popular films always attracted large audiences, but even older productions attracted larger audiences than might be expected. The cinema was also the only place where people could watch newsreels and keep up to date with events in the war, although there was a healthy scepticism over official censorship and just how much information was actually released. Listening to the wireless broadcasts of the BBC also remained a popular form of relaxation. For those seeking live entertainment, the Empire Theatre and others offered variety shows which featured a wide variety of wartime acts ranging from snooker displays to music-hall comedians.

The evening of Sunday 13 October was clear with a bright moon and people in Middlesbrough were out and about, either going for a walk, going to and from work or to the pub or cinema. The sirens began to wail, but it seems that few took cover immediately. At least one bomber had snuck through the defences and at least four, but probably more, sticks of bombs were dropped. The targets appear to have been the Dorman Long works and the railway sidings, but these were missed and the bombs instead fell in the closely packed terraced housing of the Marsh Road-Argyle Street area. The devastation was terrible, with massive property damage. A total of twenty-one people were killed and many more injured, more than thirty of them seriously. Almost 600 people were made temporarily or permanently homeless.

Three steel tubing community shelters suffered direct hits and there were seven fatalities within them. One bomb fell between the shelters which stood on wasteland on Farrer Street and Marsh Road. A massive crater was left by the bomb and the blast blew out the ends of the shelters and destroyed every house on the two streets. A boxing gym and stadium on Farrer Street was also destroyed. The third shelter to be hit was on land at the corner of Hatherley Street and Benjamin Street and once again there was severe damage to nearby properties. Given the blast damage, it appears likely that these may not have been bombs but early forms of parachute mines.

Tragic stories emerged from the aftermath of the bombing and the rescue workers who were tasked with digging out those who had been buried witnessed some terrible sights. At one of the shelters, rescue workers found a man who had tried to protect a baby under his body, both were dead. At another shelter a woman and her three children had a lucky escape when they were blown out of the shelter but were unhurt, while others sitting next to them were killed. Upon arriving at a demolished row of houses, rescue workers found a small and begrimed dog scratching at a pile of debris. The rescue workers worked through the night and all night the dog remained on guard. The rescue workers feared the worst but eventually the dog's mistress, a little girl, was located and reunited with her pet.

Fatalities in Raid of 13 October 1940

Name	Age	Location
Ashfield, Walter	37 yrs	49 Farrer Street
Butterwick, William	70 yrs	Argyle Street
Carney, Francis William	44 yrs	Marsh Road Shelter
Davies, Ellen	49 yrs	Outside 1 Hardman Street
Davies, William	20 yrs	Hatherley Street
Fenton, Richard Henry	20 yrs	Hatherley Street Shelter

Name	Age	Location
Gilgallon, John	5 yrs	Marsh Road Shelter
Hawthorne, Victor	21 yrs	Farrer Street Shelter
Kay, Ellen	52 yrs	Marsh Road Shelter
Mitchenson, George James	18 yrs	97 Lord Street (died in hospital)
Riley, Rhoda	4 yrs	Marsh Road Shelter
Riley, Thomas William	8 yrs	Marsh Road Shelter
Sherwood, Margaret	27 yrs	Hatherley Street
Wileman, Ellen	44 yrs	51 Farrer Street
Williams, Maud Mary	14 mos	101 Hatherley Street
Wilson, Francis Henry	33 yrs	24 Benjamin Street
Wilson, Violet Francis	29 yrs	24 Benjamin Street
Wood, Catherine	86 yrs	Marsh Road
Cronin, John Joseph	10 yrs	18 Benjamin Street (died in hospital)
Emmerson, Mary Jane	59 yrs	168 Marsh Road (died in hospital)
Smitheringale, Elizabeth	14 yrs	162 Marsh Road (died in hospital)

It would appear that there was also an incident on Newport Road, as two men died there within days. Mr Richard Nightingale (57) died at 116 Newport Road on 18 October and three days later an AFS man, Hugh Robb (43), died in the same street. There is no record of a bombing on these dates, so it is possible that the two were killed in the raid of 13 October, but their bodies not discovered until later.

Many Middlesbrough men who volunteered for the Royal Navy found themselves in the Royal Naval Patrol Service serving alongside men who had worked aboard trawlers before the war and were members of the Royal Naval Reserve (RNR). The trawlers were usually engaged upon minesweeping and anti-submarine warfare service, but were also pushed into operating patrols of the vital sea lanes. The bulk of the trawlers were civilian vessels taken over by the Admiralty, but others were purpose-bult naval trawlers which were built along civilian lines and outfitted for naval service. A great many trawlers were lost during the war and the men aboard them paid a very high price. In October, two Middlesbrough sailors lost their lives while serving aboard such trawlers. HMS *Lord Stamp* was a fairly modern example of a trawler which had been pressed into Admiralty service as an anti-submarine warfare vessel. The 448-ton vessel had been completed in the summer of 1935, but on 14 October 1940 she hit a mine while off the Dorset coast. Among the casualties was Stoker 2nd Class Francis Waite, a 23-year-old Middlesbrough native. Eight days after the loss of the HMS *Lord Stamp* the naval trawler HMS *Hickory* was also mined close to the site of the sinking of the previous vessel while off the Isle of Portland, Dorset. The Tree-class trawler sank with the loss of twenty-four of her crew, including Stoker 2nd Class Albert Daniel Parker (26). Just over a week after the two trawlers had been lost off Dorset, another Middlesbrough man lost his life aboard yet another trawler. Many of the trawlers pressed into service had been at sea for many years and the HMS *Tilbury Ness* was one such case, with the 279-ton vessel having been launched at the height of the First World War in 1917. On 1 November the trawler was hit by bombs and sunk in the Thames Estuary with the loss of ten of her crew, including another Middlesbrough Stoker, William Alexander Grainger.[20]

The surge in accidents during the hours of blackout claimed another victim on 3 November when Mr James Rickards (43) of 61 Ayresome Street died in hospital after being hit and killed by a bus. At the coroner's inquest the bus driver, Mr Norman Harvey of 3 Victoria Road, explained how he had been driving a bus along Albert Road at approximately 9:20 pm on the night in question when a dark shape suddenly appeared in front of the bus and he heard a thump. Immediately stopping the bus, Mr Harvey got out and found that he had hit someone. He testified that he had been doing no more than 10–15 mph at the time of the collision and had no warning or time to brake. Mr Rickards was taken to hospital but died early the next morning. The coroner recorded a verdict of accidental death but added his concerns that many pedestrians in the town were not exercising sufficient caution when crossing busy roads in the darkness.

Middlesbrough's determination to continue to raise money for the war effort continued throughout the year and by the start of November the town had raised £1,456,156 which averaged at more than £10 per head of population. In the week ending 2 November more than £22,000 had been raised thorough investment in National Savings. The Middlesbrough Emergency Relief Fund which had been launched and championed by the Mayor (Councillor Sir W.H. Crosthwaite) had nearly reached the sum of £10,000. Donations both large and small had come in from a very wide variety of Middlesbrough's population. In the first week of November, for example, Ind. Coope and Allsopp Ltd. had donated £100, while the workmen of Pease and Partners, Normanby Ironworks, had contributed £14.

While the vast majority of people in Middlesbrough were firmly committed to the war effort, there were still some who took advantage of wartime conditions to undertake criminal actions for their own profit. On 8 November, Middlesbrough Police Court heard the case of Norman Patrick Wilson of Aske Road, who had been charged with having stolen two coats from the Clarence Club on Southfield Road. Wilson told the court that he had taken the items while drunk and had no intention of stealing. This excuse was not one taken seriously by the court after the chief constable revealed details of Mr Wilson's previous convictions and the accused was duly found guilty and sentenced to two months' hard labour.

Another man sent to prison at Middlesbrough was far more to be pitied. William Murray, described as an old, bearded man, of no fixed abode, had called at a house seeking alms but had unfortunately chosen the home of a particularly hard-hearted War Reserve Police Constable who had arrested him for begging. Mr Murray had a long history of begging and so was sentenced to one month, although the presiding magistrate declared that he had been unfortunate.

In November the York Assizes heard the case of a murder in Middlesbrough. On 11 August Mr Edward Scollen (42) had been arrested and charged with the murder of his estranged wife, Beatrice Barbara Scollen. The couple had an unhappy marriage and it seems further strain was placed upon it by the fact that Mrs Scollen had been married twice previously and had four children.[21] At the end of July she had left her husband, who had also been previously married and had three children, and gone to live with a relative. On the afternoon in question Scollen had been drinking heavily. He then approached his wife and spoke to her about who would be responsible for caring for the children. This led to an argument in which Mr Scollen told his wife that if she would not live with him she would not live with anyone either. Mr Scollen then produced a pocket knife and struck his wife three times. She tried to get away but he caught up with her and dragged her into the street where she collapsed. One of the knife blows had penetrated her heart. Scollen afterwards tried but failed to take his own life. After deliberating for over one hour the jury returned a guilty verdict and Mr Scollen was sentenced to death. Scollen subsequently had an application for an appeal turned down and on Christmas Eve he was hanged at Durham Prison.

One of the issues which developed from the vastly increased military presence in the Middlesbrough area was the judgement by some that a significant percentage of young women were letting their moral standards slip by hanging around military bases and establishing casual sexual relationships with members of the services. One group that seemed to be particularly concerned about this issue was the Middlesbrough East Labour Party. The constituency party also expressed concern about a growing suicide rate among women and a perceived rise in cases of indecent assaults committed against young women. To attempt to ameliorate these issues, the party urged the local police to consider appointing full-time female police officers, believing that women could deal better with the issues causing these problems. By the beginning of November, however, these entreaties had been met with rejections by the chief constable. In the first week of November, the chief constable met with a deputation from the constituency party and told them that while he was not against the employment of women in the police, he did not believe that the 'present time was opportune'.[22] He added that the deputation had held some views which were not accurate, in that they believed female officers would be able to persuade women who were at risk of placing their morals in danger to go home. This, he claimed, was not so. Mr Edwards said that the deputation did not seem to realise that the police had no power to interfere with a subject's liberty unless an offence was being committed.

As evacuees continued to return to Middlesbrough the council was forced to consider the expense of providing further air raid protection to schools which were in the evacuated areas of town. It was estimated that the cost of providing the extra protection would come to over £11,000 and the Finance Committee proposed applying for permission from the Ministry of Health for the total amount.

As the year progressed the Home Guard had begun to undertake more tasks as training and equipment improved and the people of the area came to accept, and even appreciate, the efforts of these once largely ridiculed volunteers. In early November the North Riding Territorial Association met with the Lord Lieutenant, Lord Bolton, in the chair. At the meeting the growing importance of the force was emphasised and it was stated that within the next few days all the Home Guard units in the North Riding, including Middlesbrough and the surrounding area, would have received their issue of either battledress or denim uniforms.

More good news for the Home Guards was the announcement that the men of the North Riding would receive free medical care for any injuries suffered on duty. The British Medical Association (BMA) had approached the War Office and suggested this scheme, and it had been agreed that four medical centres would be set up in the North Riding, including one at Middlesbrough.

Throughout the final two months of 1940 the losses of men in the Merchant Navy continued to mount and a number of Middlesbrough families lost loved ones. Typical of these losses was OS Redvers Barnard. OS Barnard was the 21-year-old son of Frank and Edith Barnard, and a native of Middlesbrough.[23] On 22 November he was serving aboard the SS *Bradfyne*, a 4,740-ton steam merchant owned by the Cardiff firm of Sir William Reardon Smith & Sons Ltd. The ship was off the west coast of Ireland and nearing the end of its voyage as part of Convoy SC-11 from Sydney, Canada, to Belfast, with a cargo of 4,500-tons of maize when, at 1.17 am, she was struck amidships by a torpedo fired from *U-100*. The damage to the ship was fatal and she sank quite quickly with the loss of thirty-nine of her crew. Two days later four survivors were picked up in a lifeboat.

The A-class destroyer HMS *Acheron* had played a role right throughout the Norwegian campaign before being put on Channel escort duties. She had been damaged in July and sent to Portsmouth for repairs, but while there, on 24 August, she had suffered more damage during an air raid and the repairs were not completed until the end of November. At the beginning of December the destroyer put to sea for trials and on 17th of that month she was sailing in night trials off the Isle of Wight and was at full speed when she hit a mine. The explosion caused severe structural damage to the bow and the speed of

SS Bradfyne. (City of Vancouver Archives)

the destroyer took her under within four minutes. There were 215 men aboard, including a number of dockyard workers, but only nineteen survivors. Among the dead were forty-five dockyard workers and 151 crew. The dead included at least one Middlesbrough man, Supply Assistant Robert Harper (21).[24]

The Germans, as we have seen, went to great efforts to plant mines inside British harbours and in the approaches. An especial effort was made to seed the Thames Estuary with mines and these caused the loss of many ships. On 17 December, John and Florence Richardson of Teesville, Middlesbrough, were no doubt preparing for, and looking forward to, their second wartime Christmas, unaware that their 24-year-old son, Stoker 1st Class James William Richardson, had been killed aboard the boom defence vessel HMS *Robert Connolly*. The 1918-vintage trawler had struck a mine off Sheerness and sunk with the loss of seventeen of her crew.[25]

CHAPTER 3

1941 – Slogging On

In November 1940 the Tees Side Bridge & Engineering Works Ltd had taken over the Cleveland dockyard, a disused shipyard which had formerly been owned by Raylton Dixon, so that the firm could move into other fields of construction. Orders had been placed for the construction of tank landing-craft and it was in the early months of 1941 that the first vessels were assembled and launched. These vessels were first fabricated at the bridge yard before being moved in individual pieces to the Cleveland dock where they were assembled and fitted out before being launched and tested prior to commissioning into service.

One early launch did not go quite to plan, however. The first tank landing-craft to be launched went down the slipway without problems, but as it was departing from the dockyard to the resounding cheers of the workforce from the yard it began to circle uncontrollably. The circle that the vessel ascribed led to it return back to its launch site, much to the embarrassment of the watching managers and workforce. It was quickly discovered that the triple screws which drove the vessel had all been fitted so that they turned in the same direction and this had resulted in the problem. The issue, one which was probably the result of a lack of experience of vessel construction, was quickly rectified.

Head Wrightson & Co. at Thornaby were also busy during this period. The firm, which specialised in heavy engineering, was turning its hand to the production of bombs, sea mines and armoured cars in addition to other products. It was this type of contribution to the war effort which made the Teesside area so strategically valuable.

ICI, both at Billingham and at its scattered shadow factories, was producing fuel and chemicals which were of vital importance to the war effort. At one shadow plant at Clitheroe in Lancashire a catalyst was

A Tank Landing Craft being tested on the Tees. (Teesside Archive)

made which enabled high octane fuel to be produced, this later enabled the Spitfire and other types of aircraft to increase their top speeds so that in 1944 the V1 flying bombs could be intercepted.

Among the lessons learned as a result of the early air raids on Middlesbrough was that the many rescue squads in the town needed better facilities. As a result of this, four depots were opened during the year. These were at Acklam Road, on land donated by the Co-operative Society, in Park Road South, next to St Joseph's Church, in Green Lane, next to St Mary's Church Hall, and in Cargo Fleet Land, across the road from the Brambles Farm Hotel.

Another important lesson was that fires caused by incendiary bombs needed to be fought as quickly as possible if larger fires were not to become established. Thus, volunteers were enrolled to become firewatchers who would remain in place during raids, looking after business premises and other important unmanned properties. The administrative and training organisation of such a force was a massively complicated undertaking but one which showed itself to be of particular value during subsequent air raids, despite the danger it placed the volunteers in.

The Stockton-based joinery firm of F. Hills & Son Ltd was still manufacturing Jablo propeller blades at its Manchester factory as well as in Stockton but the latter factory had also begun to manufacture aeronautical plywood, which was produced in sections less than 1mm in thickness. The successful development and testing of the De Haviland Mosquito, dubbed the 'wooden wonder', and its purchase by the Air Ministry in large numbers, meant the demand for this aeronautical plywood increased massively. The plywood was used to provide the stressed skin of the Mosquito, which went on to perform valuable service as a bomber, fighter-bomber, night fighter and reconnaissance aircraft until its retirement in 1963. F. Hills & Son established control over twenty-six separate premises during the war, so valuable were the products it produced. These included wings for aircraft such as the Avro Anson and Airspeed Oxford as well as propeller blades for numerous types including the Spitfire and Hurricane.

One of the more bizarre experiments undertaken by F. Hills & Son was an attempt to outfit a single-engine fighter aircraft with the capacity to lift a heavy bomb slung underneath its belly by increasing the lift available on take-off. As a result, a Hurricane fighter was loaned to the firm so that a releasable top wing constructed of plywood could be added to test this theory. The plan was for the fighter to take off with the heavy bomb slung underneath and then to eject the top wing and carry on to the target. Needless to say, the plan was quietly dropped as newer, more efficient purpose-built heavy bombers were becoming available.

With the Germans making attacks in the areas of Liverpool and Manchester, a number of enemy reconnaissance aircraft flew over the Middlesbrough area in March. On the afternoon of Sunday 30 March one such aircraft, a Junkers Ju88, was pursued and shot down by a Spitfire from 41 Squadron while over Wilton Moor. Station Officer Haggath lived at Teesville and witnessed the chase and shooting-down of the bomber. He immediately went down to the fire station at South Bank football ground and, with the second-in-command of the Eston brigade of the NFS, Mr T. Marks, drove to the scene in a car. They were flagged down by some youths who told them that a German airman had come down in some nearby woods. The two men explored the woods and came across the body of a Luftwaffe airman still in his parachute harness. They turned the body over to Lieutenant P. Thompson of the local Home Guard.

Heavy air raids over the North-East, particularly Tyneside, in the spring of 1941 had focused minds on the protection of important industrial concerns in the area. The deployment of large smokescreens to hide facilities from aerial observation were pioneered on Tyneside but quickly taken up on Teesside. The large Billingham ICI plant was particularly vulnerable and a detachment of the King's Own Scottish Borderers arrived to provide protection. The soldiers were in charge of smoke-producing equipment which was mounted on lorries. The lorries would be parked on the road between Billingham and the Tees Newport Bridge or, if the wind shifted, on Haverton Hill Road. During an alert the lorries would ignite their combustion chambers which were fuelled by a mixture of oil and water, and large amounts of thick black smoke would be produced to drift over the area. The smokescreen was very effective in obscuring the plant but the smoke resulted in a terrible stench hanging over the area.

The Tees-built MS *Gladiolus* had continued to serve in the Atlantic and had successfully escorted a number of convoys, participating in attacks on a number of submarines. In September, however, she was transferred to the Newfoundland Local Escort Group led by the HMCS *Columbia*. On 16 October (the second anniversary of her keel being laid down on Teesside) she was off Iceland escorting Convoy SC-48 which was under sustained attack. At 10 pm HMCS *Wetaskiwin* received a signal which purported to come from *Gladiolus*, both ships were port-side escorts, and which requested a positional fix. The commander of HMCS *Wetaskiwin* doubted the veracity of the signal (believing it could be from a U-Boat attempting to find the convoy) and asked for, but did not receive, verification.

SC-48 consisted of thirty-eight ships in ten columns and was escorted by two separate Task Units (TU) consisting of five destroyers and four corvettes, including vessels from the Royal Navy, the Royal Canadian Navy, the Free French Navy and the US Navy. On the night of 16/17 October there was a great deal of confusion. Escort duties were just about to change, the ships of the convoy commodore and vice-commodore were lagging behind and out of touch, the different services of the escorts had differing procedures and a course change had just taken place. During the night at least five U-Boats made repeated multiple attacks on the convoy and claimed the sinking of seven merchants and a destroyer. Six merchants were lost and the USS *Kearny* had been hit and damaged, but most mysteriously of all as the morning came was the fact that HMS *Gladiolus* had vanished. Extensive enquiries were made as to the fate of the corvette, but little was learned. A detailed examination of the logs from attacking U-Boats, however, reveals that *U-553* reported a hit scored on an unknown ship at 12.07 am, just seven minutes after the purported final transmission for the corvette. No merchant ships were hit at this time and it seems very likely that a torpedo fired at a merchant ship had missed, but hit HMS *Gladiolus*. A column of flame was reported at the time this torpedo hit and it was at first assumed that a tanker had been hit, but it appears that HMS *Gladiolus* had been hit by chance, while astern of the convoy and the flames were the detonation of her magazine, which caused her to sink instantly.

The change to a total-war economy and manufacturing structure was one which had to be taken both speedily and with great care and attention to detail. One of the companies which were entrusted with overseeing the infrastructure of these developments was the Power-Gas Corporation Ltd. of Stockton. The company was placed in charge of coordinating the efforts of companies, many of which were based on Teesside and in the wider North-East, which were constructing

HMS Gladiolus *shortly after commissioning.* (Public Domain)

Bailey bridges, they also constructed several factories which produced hydrogen for the RAF, oversaw the construction of hundreds of smaller gas plants which were to provide emergency supplies and produce supplies for the many shadow factories which were being built all over the country. The company also oversaw plants used in the production of magnesium, and oversaw the immensely complicated task of reorganising and rebuilding the British mineral oil production industry.

In August there were a number of raids which hit Stockton. The area had thus far escaped fairly lightly, but just five minutes after the blackout on the night of 15 August, a single aircraft dropped five high-explosive bombs on the Blue Hall Estate. A direct hit on 160 Norton Avenue killed all seven of the occupants, and at number 116 a widow was killed. Damage to properties in Norton Avenue and several surrounding streets was heavy and a large number of people had to be accommodated. The bodies from 160 were never recovered, such was the force of the explosion. The victims at the house were Mrs Margaret Boundy aged 45 and her five sons (Alan (14), Martin (12), Edwin (10), William (7) and George (5)). The boys' father, Martin Luther Boundy, had died before the war. The other casualty in this house was Ada Jane Allen (73). Just three nights afterwards, another bomb fell on two rows of properties in Norton. Three people were killed and a further twenty-one injured.

With the increasing demand for aircrew, the training machine of the RAF increased its capacity massively during the war. The expansion of Bomber Command and Coastal Command meant that far more air gunners were required than had hitherto been the case. This was exacerbated by the decision that all aircrew would be fully qualified in their profession and would have a minimum rank of sergeant, as opposed to the early days of the war when volunteers drawn from the ranks of airmen had been much the norm. The initial training of air gunners took place at various Air Gunnery Schools (AGS) before the men moved on to Operational Training Units (OTUs), where they met up with their future crews. The training was done apace and there were many accidents in which trainee aircrew lost their lives.

RAF Llandwrog was host to 9 AGS and during the afternoon of 10 October there was a horrific accident at the airfield which took the lives of seventeen aircrew, including a very experienced Middlesbrough pilot. Two of the unit's Armstrong Whitworth Whitley aircraft were returning from a gunnery training exercise and were approaching to land. Whitley I (K7252) was being flown by the commanding officer of 9 AGS, Squadron Leader Herbert Victor Barker. The 42-year-old pilot hailed from Middlesbrough and was a very experienced officer, having been in the RAF since 1922. Squadron Leader Barker flew a standard circuit approach before coming in for landing, but unbeknownst to him Whitley I (K9041) had approached to land directly without making the usual circuit. Squadron Leader Barker saw the other aircraft below him at the last second and both aircraft took avoiding action. Barker pulled his aircraft up and to the right, but one of the propellers from the other Whitley struck his aircraft and severed the tailplane. K7252 immediately flipped onto its back and plummeted onto the airfield, bursting into flames on impact. Squadron Leader Barker was a married man who lived at Linthorpe. His family brought his remains back for burial at Middlesbrough (Acklam) Cemetery.

November saw the launch of another River-class frigate built by Smith's Dock. HMS *Rother* had been ordered in February, construction had begun at the end of June and took just five months with the frigate being launched on 20 November. Commissioned early in the next year the frigate survived the war and was responsible for liberating the last British territory to be freed from Japanese occupation, Christmas Island.

In December, the bomb-damaged ARP control centre in the Unitarian Trinity Church on Corporation Road was abandoned in favour of a purpose-built site at Sandy Flatts behind Acklam Road.

CHAPTER 4

1942 – A Year of Loss

On 15 January a small number of low-flying enemy aircraft made bomb and machine-gun attacks on a number of locations between Northumberland and Teesside, but that night the enemy came back to attack across a similarly wide frontage. Among the sights which had grown familiar to the people of Middlesbrough were those of the barrage balloons which were used as part of the town's defences; they proved their effectiveness on this evening when, at around 6.20 pm, a Dornier Do217E, which was believed to have been dropping mines, hit a balloon cable belonging to a balloon operated by 938 Squadron at Billingham. Section Officer Haggath of the NFS was on duty at a station in a disused chapel at Lorne Terrace and he heard an aircraft coming down with its engines at full power. It was obvious that the aircraft would come down nearby and Haggath took cover just before hearing the loud crash. Upon emerging, he investigated the scene and found that the Dornier had crashed onto a railway line beside Clay Lane works, leaving a very large crater; the four crew were all killed. The balloon was being flown from atop a slag tip and chunks of slag had been thrown up by the impact, landing on the roof of the fire station, but the NFS engines had escaped damage as they had been dispersed because of the alert.

As the last workers left the large furniture and drapery store owned by Messrs Binns Ltd. in Middlesbrough on the evening of 27 March smoke was seen coming from the upper windows. Inside, the manager and some firewatchers made an unsuccessful attempt to extinguish the blaze but were forced to evacuate the premises. By the time the NFS arrived the fire was very well established and spreading from the upper floors. Much of the stock was flammable and after an hour it had become clear that the store could not be saved. For over six hours some 200 firemen and women (assisted by a number of soldiers), thirty engines, three turntable ladders and ten escapes battled the flames, but by the next morning only the outer walls remained. The NFS did, however, manage to contain the blaze and saved several threatened premises including a hotel, cinema, the Corporation baths and a large café. Three firemen were slightly injured during the night and millions of tons of water were used, including supplies pumped from the dock via the static water tank on Corporation Road. The fire was the largest ever experienced in Middlesbrough.

The height of the fire at the Binns store. (Hartlepool Northern Daily Mail)

The night of 15/16 April saw the Luftwaffe active over the North-East, with bombs falling on communities ranging from Northumberland to the North Riding. In Middlesbrough a fairly sizeable raid developed with high-explosive and incendiaries being dropped over several areas of the town. A total of twenty-six people were killed while fifty-two were seriously injured. Property damage was also severe, with thirty-nine premises being destroyed and 1,700 damaged, while public utilities were also disrupted. Among the dead were eleven children under the age of 16, including three under 2 years of age. Among the dead were three men who were serving in an official capacity. Richard Brighty (63) and his son Norman (32) were both killed at Laws Street; Mr Brighty senior was a warden and his son a firewatcher. The other was Christopher Simpson, a 34-year-old Home Guard who was killed at 91 Carlow Street. The worst incidents were in Mills Street where eight people were killed, Laws Street where seven people lost their lives, and at Booth Street where a further seven were killed. Among the dead were three children from the Turley family who were killed at 39 Booth Street.

For one man who worked in the ARP control centre at Stockton, the raid brought tragedy. Mr Albert Stockwell had a senior position in the centre (and later went on to become Town Clerk of Thornaby), but on the night of the raid was in London to seek information from an inspection of the ARP scheme in the capital. London was attacked on the same night and Mr Stockwell witnessed the horrors of an air raid on the capital from atop a high building. After returning to his hotel he was then awoken by a telephone call in the early hours which informed him that his mother had been killed and his father badly injured in a raid on Middlesbrough, during which the family home in Mills Street had been destroyed. His father died eight days later in hospital. As terrible as this was, the situation could have been even worse for the Stockwell family, as Albert's wife had invited her sister-in-law, who lived with her parents in Mills Street, to their home for the night.

Dead from Air Raid on 15/16 April 1942

Name	Age	Address	Notes
Bennett, Arthur	9 yrs	25 Mills Street	
Brickless, Ruth	34 yrs	52 Laws Street	
Brighty, Norman	32 yrs	Laws Street, Middlesbrough	Fire Guard
Brighty, Richard	63 yrs	Laws Street, Middlesbrough	Air-Raid Warden
Fewster, James	51 yrs	50 Laws Street	
Godsmark, George Henry	64 yrs	58 Laws Street	
Godsmark, Tama Cissie Lavinia	59 yrs	58 Laws Street	
Hagan, Hazel	11 mos	24 Orwell Street	
Horner, Agnes McGowan	70 yrs	37 Booth Street	
Horner, John Robert	15 yrs	37 Booth Street	
Kirby, Mary Agnes	21 yrs	37 Booth Street	
Leadle, John	21 yrs	37 Booth Street	
Rea, Anthony Victor	2 yrs	27 Mills Street	
Rea, Vincent Dominic	3 yrs	27 Mills Street	
Shields, Sarah Jane	75 yrs	4 Mills Street	
Simpson, Christopher	34 yrs	91 Carlow Street	Home Guard
Smithson, Dorothy	16 mos	27 Mills Street	
Smithson, Margaret Mary	21 yrs	27 Mills Street	
Stockwell, Arthur Lee	66 yrs	23 Mills Street	
Stockwell, Jenny	65 yrs	23 Mills Street	
Taylor, Bryan Tinkler	16 yrs	27 Mills Street	
Turley, Brenda	5 yrs	39 Booth Street	
Turley, Leslie	8 yrs	39 Booth Street	
Turley, Wilfred	7 mos	39 Booth Street	
Williams, William Beresford	15 yrs	24 Orwell Street	
Wright, Evelyn	32 yrs	56 Laws Street	

Bombs also hit Bell Street and incendiaries were scattered over a wide area of the vicinity. One member of a rescue squad, Mr Reginald Hebden, remembered that his squad arrived at Bell Street under a shower of incendiary bombs, to find one house ablaze. Three men were desperately carrying furniture from the house despite the fact that the house had suffered extreme structural damage. They refused to stop until a policeman ordered them to as they attempted to remove a piano. In the shop next door to the house a woman was trying to salvage bags of sugar from the flames and had to be restrained by the rescue squad. An auxiliary fire pump then arrived with six firemen, but when they turned on the water the jet hit an electrical fitting and the shock running down the water stream knocked out all six of the firemen and disabled the pump.

The next day, Mr Hebden was part of the second squad and was sent to look for missing people in Mills Street. Upon arrival they were told to begin searching the remains of three houses which had been completely destroyed, as it was believed a woman was missing. A search had already been carried out during the night but nothing had been found and so Mr Hebden spoke to the missing woman's husband, who was an ARP warden. The warden told him that he had just left the house to go on duty when the bomb exploded, his wife had been getting dressed before going to the shelter and he believed she was still in the bedroom when the bomb fell. Armed with this information the rescue squad decided to start digging down from the top of the rubble, but the pile was unstable and could not take much weight. Against regulations, the squad asked a passing messenger boy to go to the top and remove the rubble brick by brick. He had only been doing this for a few minutes when he called Mr Hebden to him and pointed out a foot in the wreckage. The boy was quickly sent to get a cup of tea while the rescue squad completed the task of removing the woman's body.

With Middlesbrough recovering from the latest bombing there was further sad news as the news of more local war casualties arrived. The SS *Norman Prince* had been the first wartime launch at the South Bank yard of Smith's Dock Co. Ltd., but the ship had a short life. In the early hours of 29 May, the steam merchant was sailing (in ballast) between Columbia and St Lucia when, off Martinique, she was hit in the engine room by a torpedo fired from *U-156*. The ship lost all power and began to settle. Damage had been done to several of her lifeboats and there was some panic on board. Some ten or so escaped in the remaining lifeboat but a number of men were left aboard. As these men were struggling to release life rafts the U-Boat fired a coup-de-grace and the ship sank very quickly, suffering a boiler explosion as it slipped under. The Master and thirteen crew were lost.

Middlesbrough service personnel found themselves posted far from home during the war and for those in relationships this placed further strain upon them. At the end of April there had been a particularly tragic occurrence when a Middlesbrough lorry driver, William Latham (24), had gone to Rosyth where his fiancée was stationed with the Women's Royal Navy Service (WRNS) and had stabbed her to death. The victim, Jean McBurney, was herself from Middlesbrough. Mr Latham's defence claimed that their client was insane and had been at the time of his defence and that his condition meant that he was unable to give

The SS Norman Prince. (Public Domain)

directions for his own defence. The trial took place at Perth High Court on 3 June and expert testimony was given by Professor David K. Henderson as to Mr Latham's mental balance. He testified that Mr Latham had told him was very devoted to the victim and that after he had been turned down on medical grounds for both the Army and Royal Air Force had experienced trouble sleeping and had become obsessed with McBurney. Professor Henderson also testified that during his interview Mr Latham had at times wept, laughed and at times burst into song. Another expert witness, Dr W.M. McAllister testified that in his view the turning down of Mr Latham by the services had led to a feeling that he was being treated and looked at with contempt. This feeling had been compounded when his fiancée was accepted for service. The insanity plea was duly accepted and Professor Henderson's testimony that 'this unfortunate impulsive attack appears to have been determined by suspicion, jealousy and revenge'.[1] Lord Moncrief therefore ordered that Latham be detained in prison at His Majesty's pleasure.

Just weeks after the above murder there was another shocking murder involving Middlesbrough. On the night of Saturday 13 June the police were summoned to Sutton Hall (the 18th century manor house which was the residence of Major and Mrs G.H. Peake) in Thirsk. Upon arrival, Sergeant Duck found a 16-year old pantry boy in blood-soaked pyjamas. Another pantry boy, 15-year old Clive Green of Burnsville Road, Grangetown, lying unconscious on his bed with multiple wounds to the face and chest. Nearby was a discarded game carving knife and a poker. Green died before medical aid could reach him and the unnamed youth was arrested on suspicion of murder. Appearing before Thirsk Juvenile Court on 15 July he pleaded not guilty and the case was remanded to the assizes. The case subsequently came before York assizes on 12 November but the unnamed pantry boy who was accused of the crime had been found to be insane and unfit to plead. He was therefore kept in custody at the King's pleasure.

On 17 June a fire broke out at the premises of E. Upton & Sons Ltd. on Linthorpe Road. Despite the best efforts of the NFS the store was destroyed. The following day the police and NFS were alerted to a blaze at the premises of Dickson & Benson Ltd. (furnishers and grocers). The fire spread extremely quickly and the police, aided by soldiers and members of the public evacuated people from nearby properties. Despite the strenuous efforts of the NFS, which deployed fifty engines and pumps, the fire continued to spread and eventually covered an area of some 4,000 square yards and consumed the premises of Binns Ltd., Saltmers drapers, Anthony Donald, hosier, Mason & Sons (jewellers), Maypole Dairy Co., W.H. Smith & Sons, Charles, costumer, and Mansfield and Sons, boot dealers. The property of Dickson & Benson's was completely gutted with only the walls and tangled remains of ironwork left, while the other properties were all destroyed or very seriously damaged (Binns, it may be recalled, had suffered a serious fire at a neighbouring store just months previously). Several cottages in Dundas Street were also damaged in the blaze. The residents were evacuated and the homeless were put up at Hugh Bell Schools. Three police officers were injured and several firemen had lucky escapes when walls collapsed at the front and rear of the property of Messrs Dickson & Benton. It took many hours to get the blaze under control and the damage was put at over £1,000,000.

The police quickly linked the blazes of 17 and 18 June with three smaller fires which had been started at stores in the same neighbourhood and on 20 June a 13-year-old boy was apprehended. Three days later the boy was brought before the Juvenile Court in Middlesbrough where he was charged with four counts of having caused malicious damage. At the beginning of the case the boy's representative, Mr Laurieston, said he would prefer the boy to plead not guilty. The chief constable, Mr A.E. Edwards, argued that the boy should be named, but this was turned down with the court declaring that it was not common practice and was not in the public interest. It had also been established that a younger brother of the boy had not been responsible for any of the fires. Giving evidence, the chief constable stated that upon being apprehended the boy immediately confessed, and so that there could be no doubt the

The height of the blaze at Dickson & Benson Ltd. (Newcastle Journal)

police subsequently took him to the sites of the fires and he accurately identified where he had started the blazes. On the days in question he had been going around the stores in Linthorpe Road collecting wood to be resold as firewood. He stored the wood in a pram and this was seen at the sites of all the fires. Furthermore, the boy's headmaster told the court that on both days the boy had been late and was marked as being absent. Detective Inspector Grimes gave evidence that the boy had told him that, in respect of the most serious fire, he had seen a door ajar at Dickson & Benson, and that he had thrown a match into a crate from which crockery had just been unpacked. The boy also said that he did not think his actions would result in such a large fire.

In the face of such evidence Mr Laurieston could do little, but he did seek to represent the boy in as good a light as possible, telling the court that his family had been shocked and deplored their son's actions. Actions which, as he admitted, had disastrous consequences to the town and district. Mr Laurieston also said that he had questioned the boy himself and was satisfied that he was telling the truth and was not lying to try to look impressive. He also informed the court that the boy's father had taken a sensible view of the matter and had 'agreed in view of the malicious propensities of his son, that he should be sent to some place where he can be disciplined and kept under supervision'.[2]

The court also heard that the boy had previously been brought before them in 1937 charged with warehouse breaking and had been placed on probation. Despite his obvious shortcomings, the boy's school character and conduct was described as good. Alderman Brown summed up, saying that it seemed obvious that the boy had become obsessed with setting places on fire and that he had caused hundreds of thousands of pounds of damage in following this drive. Mr Lauriestone, however, said that the boy had no abnormalities and was merely lacking from adequate discipline. After consulting, the bench sentenced the unnamed boy to committal to an approved school; he was placed in a remand home until arrangements could be made.

Throughout 1942 the Luftwaffe made a series of attempts to raid the Middlesbrough area. The raids themselves were fairly small with limited numbers of aircraft involved. On the night of 6/7 July some twenty bombers attacked the Tyne/Tees area. At 1.45 am the Billingham ICI plant was hit with both HE and incendiaries. The plant was a key target and the first aircraft also dropped flares so that others could target the site. Over the course of the next hour, seventeen separate fires were started in the site. One of the most serious incidents was when an oil tank suffered a direct hit and millions of tons of petrol were lost. One of the plant's firemen, Mr John Dowd (61), was killed while attempting to stem the blazes. As a result of the damage, production was reduced to two-thirds of normal.

The bombing spread beyond the plant itself and into the occupied area around it. On the Belasis Estate several dozen houses were destroyed or damaged while the Synthonia Club Theatre and the Boys' Club on Cowpen Lane were both destroyed and a massive crater, possibly the result of a parachute mine, was left in the nearby cricket pitch. In Chiltern Avenue numbers 9–12 were destroyed along with 18–20 Rawlinson Avenue, while properties in The Green, the Tibbersely, and the Windermere were all badly affected. Another target for the raid was the Furness Shipbuilding Yard at Haverton Hill. The bombing here was nowhere near as concentrated, with only three bombs falling on target. Despite this, severe damage was done. One of the bombs hit a jetty and another fell close to a ship under construction, resulting in severe damage to both the ship and to the platers' shop. The bombing was scattered across a wide area surrounding Middlesbrough with one bomber targeting an anti-aircraft position at Cowpen Bewley, Stockton. The site was manned by men from the 426 Battery, 126th Heavy Anti-Aircraft Regiment. One of the soldiers, Gunner Leslie Henry Allen, a 21-year-old from Leicester, was killed, two men were seriously wounded and nine were less seriously hurt. All of the wounded were taken to hospital for treatment, while another eight soldiers were treated on site for minor injuries. At Norton there was further damage from incendiary bombs. A worse incident was averted due to the fact that several containers of incendiaries failed to open correctly and fell in a heap on open ground, where they burned out. Finally, a barrage balloon was also shot down.

Three Middlesbrough churches were damaged during the attack. All Saints, St Aidan's and St George's Congregational. At All Saints the actions of the vicar, the Rev. S. Barker, saved the day. The vicar was on the roof of his house dealing with an incendiary when he noticed several more fall onto the church. He immediately summoned help and people from the surrounding area, along with wardens and police, managed to extinguish the fires. Middlesbrough Girls' High School was badly hit by incendiaries. The NFS arrived on the scene to find the caretaker, Mr H. Richardson, and two teachers, Miss R.N. Barker and Miss M.V. Pearse, tacking the blaze with stirrup pumps. The building, however, was badly damaged and the fire resulted in the pupils being transferred to other schools. Eight young people, all of them aged under 18, also became heroes when they saved the Co-operative Society premises, including the Victoria Hall, on Linthorpe Road by fighting fires started after incendiaries fell through the roof.

Remarkably, casualties were few. The only fatality was Mr Dowd, while only three people were badly injured (including a reserve police officer who was hit by an incendiary bomb) and six more slightly injured.

A smaller number of bombers returned the next night, targeting Billingham and Middlesbrough once more. Several of the bombers managed to penetrate the barrage balloon screen around Billingham, although one struck a cable and had to jettison its bombs, injuring several WAAF balloon operators. Oil tanks at Billingham Reach Wharf were hit early in the attack and the blaze attracted other bombers to the area. The fire was later smothered in foam and left to burn for the rest of the week. Four bombs at Billingham Bottoms seriously damaged electric cables and this resulted in difficulties for the ARP reporting organisation. The ICI plant at Billingham was once again targeted by flares and on this night it was hit by a number of HE and incendiaries in a short raid of less than three-quarters of an hour. Despite the short period some twelve fires were started, two of them being classed as serious fires, reducing output still further. The destruction of the oil tanks also affected production at ICI. Special Constable William Frank Appleton (50) was on duty as a dispatch rider on this night. The impact of nearby bombs caused him to lose control of his motorcycle and he died of his injuries four days later in Stockton and Thornaby Hospital. Constable Appleton was a married man, and had lived with his wife, Blodwen Appleton, at 40 Howard Crescent, Haverton Hill-on-Tees. His father was George Appleton, a Justice of the Peace who lived at 94 Station Road, Billingham.

Property damage was once again severe with forty-nine houses destroyed or seriously damaged and a further forty-five being damaged less seriously. The most serious damage was in Bilsdale Avenue (where seven houses were destroyed); Belasis Avenue (where six were destroyed); Cleveland Avenue and Howard Terrace (five apiece);

Durham Avenue; Harrow Road; Howard Avenue and Poplar Terrace (four apiece); and one house in each of Roscoe Road, Leven Street and Farndale Road. The most serious incident of the night occurred at 27 Cleveland Avenue where Mrs Amy Tennant (31), her two sons, John Derek (3) and Frank (2), her sister, Margaret Shepherd (38), and her niece, Marjorie Shepherd (16), were all killed. Other fatalities were Mary Alice Cockburn (51), killed at 46 Belasis Avenue, and Florence May King (28) at 44 Belasis Avenue.

In Middlesbrough itself there was more damage to houses and to several industrial concerns. Factories and warehouses near Dents Wharf suffered damage, as did the Cargo Fleet Works, at which there was a further fatality when Herbert Richard Thompson (52) was killed. With this being the second night of raiding on the area the defences were more prepared and at least two of the raiders were shot down. A Dornier Do217 was shot down into the sea off Middlesbrough by a Bristol Beaufighter of 406 Squadron, while another Dornier crashed into the sea off the Dutch coast.

Thousands of incendiaries were dropped on these two nights and the NFS were at full stretch to cope with the many fires which were started, more than fifty of which were deemed serious enough to require NFS attendance.

On the night of 25/26 July, Middlesbrough suffered its worst raid of the war when repeated waves of Luftwaffe bombers attacked the town, dropping some twenty-eight tons of bombs in total. The devices dropped included high-explosive, oil and incendiary bombs, and damage to property was very heavy, while sixteen people were killed. Reports afterwards stated that seventy-six business premises and sixty-eight houses had been destroyed, while damage had been caused to 220 business properties and 1,000 houses. The brunt of the attack fell on the area around Wilson Street and Linthorpe Road. One of the first properties to be hit in this area was the Leeds Hotel which stood at the corner of the two streets. The property was completely destroyed and the landlord, Reginald Kimberly Wray (41), his wife, Elizabeth

Milicent (42), and their maid, Margaret Farrell (20), along with an air raid warden, Howard Blakeman (58), were all killed. The damage at the hotel was so severe that some of the bodies were not recovered until four days later.

At the corner of Wilson Street and Albert Road a group of firewatchers had a fortunate escape. They had just departed the shop where they based themselves to go to the offices for which they were responsible, when a heavy bomb fell and destroyed the shop along with eight or nine others.

The most serious fire of the night was on Linthorpe Road when the Co-operative Society premises, which had been saved earlier in the month, were set on fire. Councillor Frederick Pette, the general manager of the Co-op and also a divisional air raid warden, was on duty on that night. Councillor Pette was on his way to his headquarters when his car was blown off the road by a nearby bomb blast. Fortunately, Mr Pette was uninjured; pulling himself together he drove his car back onto the road and made for the Co-op buildings after hearing that they were on fire. Upon arriving at the scene he found the food hall completely ablaze. He immediately ran into the burning buildings and began to throw books, important documents and money from a window to people waiting below. After salvaging these items, Councillor Pette and a team of volunteers did their best to fight the fires until the NFS arrived, but even the presence of forty fire pumps could not prevent the blaze from raging out of control and gutting the Victoria Hall. The situation worsened when a wall fell onto the neighbouring property, the Co-op Emporium, and set that ablaze too. Thankfully, a catastrophe was averted when the 200 or so people who were sheltering in the basement of the Emporium were safely evacuated and taken to other nearby shelters. The fire also engulfed the Eaton's Store and firefighting efforts were further hampered by damage which was done to one of the large static water tanks in the town.

Another serious incident occurred at the North Road premises of Theo Phillips' oil works. The firm supplied the steelworks and collieries with vital equipment. At the Lloyd Street end of the works were a large number of oil tanks, which at the time were full of oil and lubricants; two thirds of these ignited and were spectacularly destroyed, despite the efforts of twenty NFS pumps. A building in which greased hessian bags were made was also destroyed in the conflagration. Despite this blow the firm quickly organised alternative supplies and was soon back in business. Given the seriousness of the fire here, it is fortunate that the workforce was at home and there were no fatalities.

At Middlesbrough Goods Yard a number of bombs fell and incendiaries set alight to several wagons. Despite the fact that bombs were still falling in the vicinity, and that the nearby anti-aircraft guns were also firing, one of the LNER shunter drivers, Mr Arthur Bradshaw, climbed into an engine and worked throughout the raid, towing blazing wagons clear. Mr Bradshaw was later awarded the BEM for his courageous conduct.

Throughout the raid the men and women of the ARP and civil defence organisations, assisted by the Home Guard, went about their work, demonstrating great courage as the bombs fell around them. The men of the rescue squads were among them, trying desperately to extricate people from houses which had been reduced to little more than piles of bricks and rubble. The men of the rescue squads witnessed some horrific sights on this night, but there were also moments of grim humour. At one incident a rescue squad were working to recover a man who had been trapped in the rubble, with only his legs sticking out. As the squad members pulled on his legs they came away in their hands. The horror of the rescuers turned to laughter as it was revealed that the man had lost two legs in the First World War and wore artificial limbs; he was later pulled out and taken to hospital.

At the North Riding Infirmary incendiaries fell onto the roof and endangered the building. The first to react was a Dr P. Baxter, who emerged from his bedroom clad in only pyjamas and dressing gown and climbed up onto the roof before using buckets of water which were passed to him to extinguish the fires. Other firewatchers assisted the doctor in his task after gaining entry to the roof via a trapdoor. While crossing the roofs Dr Baxter fell and suffered a sprained ankle. Despite this injury, however, he was more concerned about the patients and the fact that the hospital would shortly be having to deal with incoming casualties.

As Dr Baxter worked on the first casualties to arrive at the hospital, he was notified of an urgent request for medical assistance which had come from the ARP control centre. A woman was trapped in debris in the area of Waterloo Road and needed urgent medical assistance. Dr Baxter could barely walk but insisted that he be carried on a stretcher to the scene. At the scene of the collapsed house, Dr Baxter crawled into a hole in the wreckage and managed to give a shot of morphine to an elderly woman who was trapped. Dr Baxter then tried to hobble back to the hospital – only to be loaned a bicycle by a passing policeman. Upon arriving at the hospital, he immediately began once again to treat victims of the raid.

Elsewhere in Middlesbrough the first aid service had also swung into action. At the first aid post off Newport Road, at the back of the Cannon Hotel, the female volunteers had assembled while the male stretcher bearers went out to bring in the injured. The post was in the thick of the bombing and all of its windows had been blown out, and because of this the lights could not be turned on. A decision was taken to relocate the post to the nearby cellar of Holy Cross Church and the volunteers immediately went about dressing the wounds of the injured who were quickly flowing into the post. The relocation did cause some problems, however, as it made getting patients who were stretcher cases out of the post rather difficult.

Bombs also fell in communities around Middlesbrough. The ICI plant was once again targeted. Damage was once again extensive with the Grinding Plant, the No 4 Nitric Acid Pump House, the Electrical Plant, the Phosphate Plant and the Kilns and Coal Section of the Casebourne Cement Works all being damaged during the raid. Two people, a man and a woman, were overcome by nitric acid fumes. At Haverton Hill thirty-five houses were badly damaged along with a cinema and a public shelter. One road, Oban Street, was completely blocked and electric cables brought down, and water and gas mains were damaged. At Cowpen Bewley, the decoy site which had been set up to draw bombing away from the ICI works continued to be effective and at least four bombs were dropped here with no damage or casualties.

The next morning saw scenes of devastation over the smoky town. Large contingents of ARP workers were assisted by council workers, firemen, policemen, soldiers and, for the first time in Middlesbrough, by men of the Home Guard, in clearing streets and bomb sites and in damping down fires and trying to reach those still believed trapped. One of the main duties of the Home Guard was in assisting the police in dispersing the crowds of sightseers and in controlling the traffic in the rubble-strewn streets, many of which were closed due to the suspected presence of unexploded bombs. Assessment after the raid placed the death-toll at sixteen while a further fifty people had been injured and some 200 left homeless. Once again, those who were acting in an official or volunteer ARP capacity suffered badly with a warden, a firewatcher and five fire guards all being killed.

Fatalities of Raid on 25/26 July 1942

Name	Age	Address	Notes
Blakeman, Howard	58 yrs	Leeds Hotel	
Farrell, Margaret	20 yrs	Leeds Hotel	
Wray, Elizabeth Millicent	42 yrs	Leeds Hotel	
Wray, Reginald Kimberley	41 yrs	Leeds Hotel	
Allen, Elizabeth	69 yrs	1 Waterloo Road	
Armstrong, Halliburton	42 yrs	Opposite 242 Linthorpe Rd	Fire Guard
Coley, Frank	44 yrs	Clifton Street	Fire Guard
Denning, Ernest	38 yrs	Middlesbrough	

Name	Age	Address	Notes
Grayson, George Henry D.	64 yrs	14 Aden Street	
Harris, George	36 yrs	Waterloo Road	Fire Guard
Holmes, Florence Gertrude	26 yrs	Clifton Street	Fire Guard
King, Basil Mervyn	17 yrs	Albert Terr	Air Raid Warden
Molloy, Michael Joseph	45 yrs	Linthorpe Road	
Pattison, Edward	55 yrs	3 Granville Road	
Pinkham, Hector	42 yrs	244 Linthorpe Road	Firewatcher
Pringle, Norman	42 yrs	Clifton Street	Fire Guard

At the ICI plant in Billingham the damage included the destruction of the finished product conveyer annexe at the fertiliser granulating plant, and the loss of the pumps of the nitric acid plant. It was this damage that released a cloud of nitric acid which resulted in breathing difficulties for some in the area and which overcame two people. The coal offloading plant, the kilns and several blocks of offices also suffered considerable damage from the blast of high explosive bombs. One employee at the plant remembered coming out of the shelter after the all-clear had sounded and found that thousands of small incendiary bombs had been scattered across the roads in the plant. They were removed by placing them in dumper trucks and ferrying them away.

Following the shock of what was Middlesbrough's worst raid, the population were understandably nervous of a repeat attack. Just a week later the Luftwaffe did indeed return, but this time in daylight. At 1.13 pm on 3 August, a train bound for the coast had just pulled out of Middlesbrough Station while the Newcastle-Middlesbrough express train had just finished disgorging its passengers and made its way to the sidings. The peace of this August lunchtime was suddenly shattered by the wail of the sirens followed immediately by the noise of aircraft engines and the staccato rattle of machine-gun fire as a Dornier Do217 dived out of the clouds and dropped four 500lb high-explosive bombs. Two of the bombs scored direct hits on the station. One of these bombs impacted on buildings which were used as waiting rooms, a refreshment room and guards' facilities and which lined the down platform. The other fell directly in front of the engine, which was towing the full carriages of the express train back to the platform ready for the return journey to Newcastle. The locomotive engine was completely destroyed in the blast, with one of its front buffers falling onto a house some 250 yards away. Many of the wagons and carriages were derailed and a load of heavy steel plates was thrown a short distance against a station wall.

In the refreshment room a 17-year-old boy, Charles Raymond Taylor, was killed. Charles was a member of the Air Training Corps and had hoped to join the RAF. He was the sixth member of his family to be killed in air raids on Middlesbrough during 1942. His older sister, younger brother and niece had been killed during the raid of 15/16 April along with other members of the family at Mills Street. The guard, James Fred Binks (53), who had arrived on the express train had taken the fatal decision to walk along the platform and cross the tracks in front of the train before he boarded and was also killed instantly.

The driver of the express, Mr Tommy Marsden, was still standing in the sidings when the bombs exploded and despite his horror, he ran towards the scene and helped to extricate some of the passengers. The driver, who was to take the train back to Newcastle, had been standing on the platform and had survived the explosion, but the fireman had been killed. A 17-year-old assistant at the station's bookstall had just closed up and was returning unsold newspapers when the bombs fell. She was in the subway underneath the station and emerged into the horror of the aftermath. The station was ablaze and everywhere there were twisted girders from the roof and from the rails and debris scattered throughout. A young woman who was working in the booking office next to the refreshment room had a very lucky escape. The booking office was situated in an arch and it was this that saved the office from further damage. The young clerk was just about to leave the office when some workmen came in and stopped her, saying it was unsafe. This too was fortunate as, shortly afterwards, the tiled wall of the subway that she would have used, collapsed. The workmen instead took her across the tracks and through the shattered remains of the train to safety. In addition to Mr Binks and Mr Taylor, three others who were injured at the station died later in North Riding Infirmary. Timothy Carroll (35) of 46 Berwick Hills Avenue, Brambles Farm, died the same day, as did William Farren (53) of 8 Milton Street, while George William Barrett (45) of 71 Gresham Road died in hospital the next day.

At the Hippodrome in Wilson Street an audience of 1,000, mainly made up of children and the elderly, crowded to watch a matinee performance of *How Green Was My Valley*. The air raid warning was broadcast at the front of the cinema but surprisingly, given the recent raids, most people decided to ignore it. Daylight raids, of course, were very unusual. The sound of the detonations stilled the audience, but the manager of the cinema made an announcement that the explosion was that of an unexploded bomb from a previous raid. One of the other bombs had in fact fallen and exploded in Crown Street just 50 yards from the cinema.

The remaining bomb fell on Station Street, demolishing a warehouse used to store fruit. Two people were killed here. Mr William Henry Thorneloe (73) of 23 Bush Street, Linthorpe, was killed at Station Street Chambers while Mr Solomon Peter Niman (34) died at 3 Station Street. The final casualty list was seven dead, with twenty-one injured and hospitalised, and thirty-five more suffering from less serious injuries.

Among those less seriously injured was Sarah 'Sally' Davis, a young woman from Blyth, Northumberland. Miss Davis had spent a short holiday with her family in Acklam and was boarding the train for Newcastle on her way back home. She had been escorted back to the station by several members of her family, including 10-year-old James Henwood. When the bombs exploded James, his mother and brother, had run away before they returned to seek his Aunt Sally. She had last been seen walking along the platform and it was on the wreckage of the platform that they found her being tended to by a soldier. Thankfully, Miss Davis had suffered only shock and was able to return to Acklam with her family.

At the offices of the *Evening Gazette*, the newspaper's chief photographer, Mr E. Baxter, had just gone into the canteen at the top floor of the building on Borough Road when he saw the aircraft dive and the bombs explode. Mr Baxter immediately left the building, jumped in a car and travelled to the scene. After taking his photographs he rushed back to the office – to be told-off for puncturing the car tyres on the broken glass – and had the photographic plates hurriedly developed before sending them to London to be inspected by the censor before being published.

The incident was not immediately reported as the censors forbade it, but when reports were published nearly a month later they highlighted the remarkable fact that the damage, substantial though it was, had caused little delay in rail operations. Goods traffic was quickly diverted while repairs were speedily carried out and freight traffic was once again going through Middlesbrough in just over twenty-four hours, while passengers began using the station just thirty hours after the bombing.

The photographs taken by Mr Baxter were published some five weeks after they had been taken but had a salutary effect. The vivid scenes captured by Mr Baxter were wired around the world and were responsible for evoking considerable sympathy for the British cause. In Australia and New Zealand the photographs even played a part in a fundraising campaign to raise money to purchase blankets, clothing and miscellaneous supplies for families who had been bombed out in Britain. The most famous photographs, some of which showed the wreckage of the train and station with the first of the dead being recovered were blown up to a 20 x 15ft enlargement and used to encourage donations.

The authorities in Middlesbrough were clearly concerned about the recent raids, but this concern resulted in what was perhaps a misjudged exercise held just four days after the bombing of the station. On 7 August the authorities decided to test how many people were still obeying the laws regarding the carrying of gas mask respirators at all times by releasing a cloud of gas which caused minor irritation among a crowd that were outside the Odeon in Corporation Street. While the test showed that at least two-thirds of the queue were not carrying their respirators the cloud of vapour, along with the minor symptoms suffered by those who did not have masks, could easily have resulted in panic and a serious situation.

A great many people still tuned in, despite repeated attempts by the authorities to discourage them, to the propaganda broadcasts that were made by the Germans, most famously by Lord Haw-Haw. On occasion these broadcasts were so amateur that they simply caused

Middlesbrough Station just minutes after the bombing. (Evening Gazette)

Repair work at Middlesbrough Station. (Evening Gazette)

amusement among listeners and a broadcast, which was heard on the night of 9 August attracted wide ridicule on Teesside when it claimed that on the previous night 'the East Anglian town of Middlesbrough' had been attacked. Not only had the town not been attacked, but the geographical inaccuracy of the broadcast claims demonstrated a naïve unprofessionalism on the part of the Germans.

CHAPTER 5

1943–1944 – Attrition

1943

By this stage of the war a great deal of work had been taken over by women. The increasing numbers of men needed in the services necessitated this, but there was also a change in attitudes among many employers as they found that women could easily be the equal of male employees and that they adapted well to the new conditions in the workplace. This was by no means absolute, as many employers still believed that women were not as valuable as male employees and there continued to be resistance in some areas, especially in the mining sector. In Middlesbrough, the many manufacturing plants required a vast input of additional labour and the vast majority of local firms took on large numbers of women workers, often employing them in heavy labour-intensive jobs which had been the preserve of men before the war.

It was not always the idea of women to seek employment, and the call up of single women aged 19–24 demonstrated that necessity drove forward the employment of women. Women who were called up were given a choice between serving in one of the female branches of the services, going into the civil defence services on a full-time basis, or of being directed into work of wartime importance (often munitions or the aircraft industry).

How, and indeed if, women benefited from the increased opportunities is hard to gauge, but in some trades women's pay did increase and in a few there was even a move towards pay equality but in many industries, such as engineering, the pay of women lagged far behind that of men. In 1943 it was estimated that the average woman employed in engineering was paid only half of what a man in the same role could expect. As industry in Middlesbrough was so heavily concentrated on engineering, this meant that the increased availability of work was a double-edged sword for women. Many of those who found work also had to balance their working hours with family life, as many were still the main homemakers and were responsible for the majority of household tasks, such as shopping.

By March, the responsibility for providing smokescreens to obscure areas of value had passed to the War Office and the Air Ministry and the use of static Haslar generators had replaced the more ad-hoc mobile units mounted on lorries manned by the Army. The smoke screens were very effective, but claims that they prevented bombers from finding the targets they protected were somewhat optimistic and some bombs continued to land on these important targets. The ICI plant at Billingham, however, had suffered what was to prove the last attack on it back in July 1942 and although the smokescreen was still called into action during alerts, no more bombs fell on the plant.

May saw the third anniversary of the formation of the Home Guard and in Middlesbrough the local units were keen to celebrate this occasion. A number of parades were held throughout the area, but the undoubted highlight was a drumhead service held in Middlesbrough on 16 May. Nearly 2,000 members of 8 and 9 Battalions of the Middlesbrough Home Guard were joined on parade by units of Home Guard anti-aircraft batteries in Albert Park. A large crowd turned out to witness the occasion. Meanwhile, in Ropner Park 1,000 officers and men from 19 Durham (Stockton) Home Guard and anti-aircraft batteries had paraded and were inspected.

As we have seen, ICI was working producing vital petrochemical and chemical products for the war effort, but the firm was also heavily involved in a rather more unusual development. Experience in France and the desert had shown that the types of infantry anti-tank weapons currently in use by the British Army were almost completely ineffective. In 1942, the War Office had issued a tender for a new weapon. Lieutenant-Colonel Stewart Blacker of the Royal Artillery was working on a hand-held version of his Blacker Bombard, but there were many difficulties and when Blacker was transferred to other duties a colleague took over his work and collaborated closely with ICI. The final product was the Projectile Infantry Anti-Tank or PIAT. The PIAT used a shaped charge warhead and, because it was based on the spigot mortar, had no back-blast to endanger its operator or to give away his position. It also possessed good armour penetration capabilities, but it did have a very heavy recoil, was difficult to reload and the shaped warhead suffered from some early unreliability. Nevertheless, the PIAT went on to become the standard infantry anti-tank weapon of the British Army and several Empire nations from its operational introduction in 1943 until 1950.[1]

Among the top-secret projects with which ICI at Billingham was involved was research into the use of heavy water (Deuterium Oxide (D_2O)), under the codename Operation Tube Alloys. Work on D_2O had been started before the war and continued apace throughout the war, as the government sought to find a weaponised use. The president of ICI, Lord McGowan, was insistent that the company should play a leading role in the development of an atomic bomb, but the discovery that a uranium gas diffusion plant, necessary for such work, would have stretched from Billingham to as far north as Durham, and as this was clearly impractical it was agreed that development should take place in

A PIAT in action, note the shaped charge round in the foreground. (Public Domain)

the USA where the wastes of the Nevada desert provided ample space which, crucially, was safe from enemy attack.

We have already heard the story of how, in 1939, Sgt William Edward Willits had become the first airman of the Second World War to be awarded the DFM. After he had completed his first tour of operations he had been posted as an instructor and was commissioned as a P/O in April 1941. After serving his period as an instructor he was posted to 233 Squadron to undertake a second tour of operations, flying the Lockheed Hudson on anti-submarine and anti-shipping strikes and patrols from Gibraltar. By April he had been promoted to F/Lt and on 6 July he was gazetted with the DFC. By this time the Middlesbrough-born airman was registered as living at Silloth in Cumbria. During his second tour of operations he had been appointed as Deputy Flight Commander and part of his DFC citation praised 'his keenness and untiring devotion to duty', by which 'he set a fine example to his squadron'. The citation also praised him for having attacked four submarines during his second tour, and on one occasion in April 1943,

> while on patrol, a U-Boat was sighted which made no attempt to submerge. Flight Lieutenant Willits engaged it with his front guns as he flew in to drop his depth charges, which straddled the submarine. The U-boat then began to submerge, but by clever manoeuvring Flight Lieutenant Willits was able to attack it again with a well-placed bomb.[2]

A key part of the ARP efforts in Middlesbrough was the placement of large static water tanks and water butts to help in the fighting of fires. When it became clear that one of the main dangers in air raids was the large numbers of small incendiary bombs which were dropped over wide areas the number of water tanks and butts was bolstered with the installation of barrels of water on many street corners.

It would seem, however, that many Middlesbrough residents were treating these potentially life-saving resources as little other than waste receptacles. By early July, the Mayor was issuing statements condemning this behaviour. The 'gross misuse of supplies of water which had been placed in various parts of the town for fire-fighting purposes' was a serious concern, and one which was going to be cracked down upon by the authorities. In the part of town north of the railway some 75 per cent of barrels had required daily attention to keep them fit for purpose. Items dumped into the barrels included bricks, empty sandbags, and dead animals. In Cannon Street and the Whinney Banks areas in the west of town the barrels were continuously being filled with filth and rubbish. Likewise, in the Grove Hill and Brambles Farm areas the barrels were being abused and in many cases barrels were being found full of rubbish just hours after they had been refilled with water. In these two areas there were also many thefts of the four-gallon tins which had been supplied with the barrels. In Cargo Fleet, a barrel was found to contain no fewer than twenty-five milk bottles, while another in Western Avenue was found to be so tightly packed with clay that it required a pick to get the clay out.

It was not only the barrels which were being misused. In the north of the town, wire guards over the top of static water tanks had been removed and rubbish thrown in. A static water tank in Marsh Road (an area which had already suffered bombing) was found to contain an old bicycle and several lamps which had been stolen from street shelters.

The chair of the Watch Committee, Councillor T. Meehan, said that the police were doing their utmost to police the barrels and tanks and that if people did not moderate their behaviour, harsher punishments would be introduced for such offences. Many had blamed children for these issues but the Mayor pointed out that this was not always the case and that in one incident four barrels had been emptied and abandoned on a busy road in the middle of the night; the offence took place between midnight and 3 am and he believed adults, possibly 'in drink', to be responsible.

Another prime concern at the time was the perceived decline in moral standards, and a meeting of the Emergency Committee heard evidence of inappropriate behaviour becoming more common inside air raid shelters, especially those which were close to public houses. The committee, therefore, urged the chief constable to ensure that a sharp look-out was kept for such offenders.

We have already seen the contribution that the Stockton joinery firm of F. Hills & Son Ltd. had on the bomber offensive with the production of the skin for the De Haviland Mosquito, but the firm also made another major contribution in 1943. The company had a small workshop off Boathouse Lane in Stockton and it was here that the company began to produce massive amounts of curious strips of aluminium foil, painted black on one side. The requirements of the sizes of these strips were demanding and none of the workers, many of them women, knew what they were producing or why. The strips of foil were codenamed 'Window', and were first used in action during the Battle of Hamburg. Dropped from the bombers of RAF Bomber Command they disrupted the radar displays of the enemy by showing a multitude of false returns, and for a time their introduction reduced losses as it temporarily paralysed the enemy night fighter force.

Another Middlesbrough firm which made a significant, though understated, contribution to the success of the war in Europe following D-Day in 1944 was Richard Hill & Co. Among the wartime work that the firm undertook was a very large order for production of Maxwelded, criss-cross, steel matting. The Air Ministry recognised that the product would prove invaluable when it was trying to rapidly establish air bases in Europe following any successful invasion. The product was also used in Britain to rapidly construct emergency landing fields for aircraft in distress.

The iron and steel-working industries in Middlesbrough and the surrounding area were, as we have seen, undertaking vital work throughout the war. In Newport the firm of Richard Hill & Co. had a large wire-making factory and the firm's specialisation in a variety of heavy-duty steel wiring resulted in a rush of wartime contracts. Not far away was the Lionweld factory, which produced steel flooring and stairs, and which during the war manufactured parts for Bailey bridges and engine parts for De Haviland. The breadth of companies involved in the metal manufacture industries in the area meant that firms large and small were constantly active in wartime production. Many firms changed their production from peacetime products to items which were vital to the war effort. This often involved investment in new machinery and the employment of additional labour. Among the smaller firms, for example, was R.W. Rundle & Co., which produced millions of steel washers during the war. These were used in a multitude of scenarios including the Mulberry Harbours used after D-Day. The shift in production types meant that the firm invested in extra equipment and took on a substantial number of extra workers, the majority of whom were women. In Stockton, Imeson & Finch Ltd turned its collective hand from peacetime production of mechanical and electrical equipment to the production of munitions components. Prime among the products that the firm made were containers for 1,000lb bombs, and for a period the firm was the only one producing these in the entirety of Britain. It was in such a manner that companies large and small in Middlesbrough and the surrounding area were to prove vital to the national war effort. The garage firm of Gerald Fleming turned its hand to wartime production too, manufacturing more than 7 million shells and bomb parts at its Trunk Road factory. Once again, the extra workforce required consisted mainly of women, with more than 260 being employed here.

Another Teesside company was one of those tasked with overseeing and organising the manufacture of the Mulberry Harbours, which were to play such a key role after D-Day. It is unsurprising, given its wartime record, that this duty fell to the Power-Gas Corporation Ltd of Stockton.

Throughout the year the Tees Side Bridge & Engineering Works yard was feverishly completing orders for a variety of landing craft. The yard had been constructing such craft since early 1941, but the pace of orders had picked up massively. These craft would be vital if the invasion of Europe was to succeed and a massive number were required.

Shipbuilding as a whole on the Tees continued to be very busy throughout 1943 and there were a number of interesting developments during the year. The Admiralty had made the decision to phase out construction of the Flower-class corvette due to its handling problems in the heavy seas of the Atlantic and to replace it with the River-class frigate. Not all shipyards were large enough to build frigates, however, and it was decided that a development of the Flower-class, known as the Castle-class, would be produced at these yards. Some ninety-five of the new class were ordered (although only forty-four would be completed). The new class looked very similar to the Flower-class but was 40ft longer and more than 200 tons heavier. The Castle-class was better armed, but was still underpowered and prone to being blown off course in high winds. Smith's Dock went on to build both frigates and corvettes.

The development of the Flower-class had attracted the attention of the French navy in 1940 and orders for four vessels had been placed. One of the ships was named *La Bastiase* and on the day that France surrendered, 22 June 1940, she had been undergoing trials when she hit a mine and sank off Hartlepool with the loss of forty-three French sailors and eighteen workers from Smith's Dock. After the loss of these valuable workers, the management at Smith's decreed that their employees would no longer accompany vessels on sea trials during wartime. In August 1943, however, this rule had to be broken in order to resolve a perplexing mystery. The HMS *Odzani* was one of the first of a number of River-class frigates to be produced by Smith's Dock, but while on trial, she was forced to return to the Tees suffering machinery trouble. It was thought that the problem had been solved, but once at sea it re-occurred and it was decided that the only way to find a solution was to send employees aboard on the next series of trials. The frigate thus left the Tees with an aerial escort and, after clearing the coastal minefields, set off on a speed run. Once again, problems were experienced. Investigations aboard revealed that grit in the starboard side shaft bearings was the problem. The grit was cleaned out and the bearings cleaned, while a sample of grit was taken to be an analysed. This analysis revealed an even more intriguing mystery, one which was potentially far more troubling.

It was found that the grit was identical to that found on the main road leading to the dockyard and the only conclusion which could be reached was that the incident was one of deliberate sabotage by unknown persons. The identity of the saboteur was never revealed and it seems that it was an isolated incident, but the motives of such sabotage were worrying. Was this the ignorant and unfeeling work of a disgruntled worker seeking to embarrass his employers, or was it something more sinister – an enemy agent or sympathiser employed in an important wartime shipyard? The question was never answered.

The Furness Shipbuilding Company at Haverton Hill had been hard at work building merchant vessels, but in 1943 the yard pioneered the building of a new class of vessel. Throughout 1942 there had been complaints that the merchant vessels being turned out were too slow and were therefore more vulnerable to attack. As a result, a new standard

HMS Odzani. (Public Domain)

for a fast cargo liner was introduced. The ships were an extension of the Empire-programme of construction and the first to be built on Teesside was the SS *Empire Chieftain*, which was constructed for the Ministry of War Transport (MoWT) and was run by Royal Mail Lines. The ships of the class were around 9,900-tons and measured 475ft in length. The SS *Empire Chieftain* served throughout the rest of the war and was part of a number of Atlantic convoys.[3]

The Furness yard specialised in tankers and during the course of the war the company was exceptionally busy constructing and launching twenty-six deep-sea tankers and sixteen coastal CHANT tankers. In addition to this the yard also produced six tramp ships and three whale factory ships. Several of the deep-sea tankers were built for the MoWT and were models which had a displacement of around 16,765-tons and were capable of 12,091-tons of fuel oil. Of the twenty vessels completed to this standard between 1943 and 1946, twelve were built at the Furness yard. In 1943, two of these ships were launched by Furness; the *Empire Bounty* at the end of September and the *Empire Law* at the end of November. At the end of the war the surviving ships of this class, along with others which were purpose-built, were transferred to the Royal Fleet Auxiliary (RFA) and renamed as Wave-class long range replenishment oilers.[4]

The firewatchers of Middlesbrough had so proved their worth that in the autumn it was agreed to extend the scheme to include firewatching street parties, who would be responsible for safeguarding their assigned street from incendiaries. This development would not have been possible if it was not for volunteers from the warden service. With their time now being freer, many wardens immediately volunteered to lead, and be a part of, firewatch street parties. The wardens became the backbone of this new force.

By this point in the war the Home Guard had become a professional and well-equipped force which undertook a wide variety of military and quasi-military tasks. The anti-aircraft defences of the area now depended largely upon the Home Guard, and they even manned the

The RFA Wave Victory. (Public Domain)

local anti-aircraft rocket batteries pioneered by their Home Guard colleagues on Tyneside. Training had also expanded and been vastly improved in comparison to the early days of the force. Regular exercises with regular troops were frequently carried out and proved valuable experience for both regulars and Home Guards. Often the Home Guards would play the role of a defensive force and would be faced with a unit from a special forces regiment, such as airborne troops. On 25 October, for example, an exercise was held across Northern Command. In Middlesbrough and Stockton, local Home Guard units guarded various vulnerable spots while the assault was undertaken by airborne troops who had marched sixty miles in the previous two days.

1944

Many people in the Middlesbrough area had followed the progress of 608 (North Riding) Squadron throughout the war and a significant number of local men served in the squadron, many of them as ground-crew. As late as February 1944 there were still seventy-nine (from an original 347) of the pre-war auxiliaries ground-crew serving. At the time, the squadron was based at Montecorvino in Italy and were flying convoy-escort patrols with the Lockheed Hudson. Of the old originals, the twelve airmen who had joined the squadron at its formation in 1930, only three remained. They were W/O Beach, W/O Harold Franklin from Norton, and Sgt William Bailey of Middlesbrough. The three men were intensely proud of their thirteen years of service with the squadron and told reporters that the same spirit still pervaded the unit, with the newer members learning from the old hands. W/O Beach proudly wore the ribbons of the British Empire Medal, the Coronation Medal and the coveted Air Efficiency Award. This final award was also worn by eight others on the squadron: W/O Franklin; Sgt Albert Brown (Thornaby); Sgt Robert Jarrett (Norton); Sgt Fred Ryder (Stockton); F/Sgt Jennison Menhennet (Billingham); LAC J. Law (Stockton); F/Sgt Sidney Kelley (Billingham); and F/Sgt Leslie Ludbrook (Billingham). The eldest of the men was W/O Jack James Thomas from Stockton who had spent twenty-four years in uniform, having previously served for eight years in the Royal Fusiliers where he spent time in France and in the Army of Occupation in Germany following the First World War. W/O Thomas told a reporter that he enjoyed being in uniform and that the only aim of the ground-crew was to keep the aircraft flying for the good officers that they had. The ground-crew also received praise from the recent commanding officer of the squadron, Wing Commander C.M.M. Grece, DFC, who praised 'these stout Yorkshiremen' as being a 'grand lot of fellows'.[5]

Sunday 14 May 1944 saw the beginning of Middlesbrough's Salute the Soldier campaign, which hoped to raise £1,000,000. The campaign was opened by the Commander-in-Chief of Home Forces and Colonel of the Green Howards, General Sir H.E. Franklyn. As part of his speech, General Franklyn read out a message from General Montgomery in which the fighting character of the Yorkshire battalions of the Green Howards was praised. General Montgomery said that the men of the

Green Howards had been with him at El Alamein, across Africa, in Sicily and in Italy. As part of the opening ceremony, the Green Howards were given the freedom of the borough in a deed which granted them permission in a ceremonial role to march through the borough and town with fixed bayonets, colours flying and bands playing. When he handed over the deed, the Mayor, Councillor R.R. Kitching, said that the town was proud of the local men who had served, or were serving, in the regiment, or who were currently prisoners of war. In replying, General Franklyn commented that it would have given him great pleasure to have organised for some Middlesbrough Green Howards to have paraded, but they were currently otherwise engaged (many were preparing for D-Day). The day, he hoped, would soon come when the men of the regiment would be able to march through the town taking advantage of the honour which had been done them in the award of the deed. When they did, he said, the 'honours of war' would be 'thick upon them'.[6] General Franklyn concluded by saying that he was well qualified to speak about the regiment as his father had joined them in 1876 and risen to command them as colonel; while he had been born into the regiment, joined it and risen to command it, while his own son was currently serving in the 6th Battalion. Despite the demands placed upon the regiment it does seem unusual that no members of the regiment turned out for the event. Part of the group of dignitaries who attended the opening ceremony were two local VCs from the First World War, Pvt Tom Dresser and Major Edward Cooper.[7]

Salute the Soldier week was slightly marred by the criminal behaviour of three Army cadets in South Bank. Police War Reserve J. Alick was investigating a light in a shop at night when he found the three cadets who had broken in. One of the boys (two were aged 15 and the other 16) raised and pointed a rifle at the officer and challenged him to 'stick 'em up'. The brave police officer grabbed the gun and the boys fled. Constable Alick caught one of them and the other two were apprehended the next day. Brought before the bench at South Bank Juvenile Court, the youths were placed on probation for having broken into the shop and into two Home Guard stores, from which they had stolen four rifles and a quantity of ammunition to the value of £61 16s. A further shop-breaking and a warehouse-breaking charge were taken into account. It was also revealed that the rifle pointed at the constable was not loaded at the time. Condition of the probation was that the boys no longer associate with one another. All-in-all the three seem to have gotten off very lightly given the circumstances.

The Salute the Soldier campaign consisted of numerous events, both large and small. These included everything from whist drives to exhibitions of military equipment and lectures on the military. In the Town Hall, a cavalcade of the history of the Green Howards from 1688 to the present day was produced and attracted a good audience. Those who were considering whether or not to donate were reminded of the sacrifices that had been made and those that were to come by Brigadier G.H. Gilmore who, at one event, told the audience, rather patronisingly, that hard fighting lay ahead and that 'our casualties will be on a scale we have not had before. We must expect them, and they will be cheerfully given if victory is won.'[8]

Throughout 1944 Smith's Dock, as a company, was kept very busy, both with construction of new ships and repairs to damaged ones. One of the more unusual orders during the year was for some large solid steel tanks for the Admiralty. The tanks, in fact, were integral parts of the ingenious Mulberry Harbours which were to be used to help supply the Allied forces after D-Day.

Furness Shipbuilding Company continued with its busy schedule throughout 1944. Included among the yard's output during the year were six more deep-sea tankers of the class described previously. Four of these were for the MoWT, while the remaining two were to enter directly into service with the RFA as Wave-class oilers. This shift in policy was down to the increased naval operations in far-flung theatres such as the Pacific. In these theatres of war the Royal Navy was expected to operate across vast distances where there were relatively few friendly ports for refuelling.

Tankers Built for MoWT and RFA at Furness Yard in 1944

Name	Pennant	Launched	Original Name	Fate
Wave Liberator	A248	9 February	Empire Milner	Scrapped 1959
Wave Commander	A244	21 April	Empire Paladin	Scrapped 1959
Wave Protector	A215	20 July	Empire Protector	Scrapped 1963
Wave Emperor	A100	16 October		Scrapped 1966
Wave Conqueror	A245	27 November	Empire Law	Scrapped 1960
Wave Governor	A247	30 November		Scrapped 1960

The Furness yard also produced a number of other vessels, including escorts and two salvage vessels which were each capable of lifting 1,500 tons. In addition to this the yard also joined in with the construction of a large number of landing craft and aided other yards by providing designs for such craft.

Among the other preparations for D-Day were plans for a pipeline under the Channel which would provide fuel supplies for the invading forces. The plan was codenamed Operation PLUTO (Pipe Line Under The Ocean). On Teesside the firm of Head Wrightson & Co. were closely involved in the project. The company also manufactured parts for the Mulberry Harbours, and was very busy manufacturing landing craft throughout the latter part of 1943 and the early part of 1944.

The announcement of the D-Day landing was met with a mixture of excitement and anxiety in Middlesbrough. Many saw this as a sign of the progress that had been made by the Allies, but with the large number of men who were serving in the front lines many families faced an anxious wait to find out the fate of loved ones who had been involved in the invasion.

In order to provide support to the landing infantry the British landed, or attempted to land, a number of armoured vehicles in the first wave. One unit manning such vehicles was the Royal Marine 1st Armoured Support Group using mainly Centaur IV Cruiser tanks armed with 95mm howitzers to take out fortified positions. It was while serving with this unit on D-Day that Marine Harold Bennison, Middlesbrough, was killed.[9] It would appear likely that Bennison's tank did not make it to the shore; he was first declared missing and his body subsequently recovered from the sea in the area of Boulogne.

With many of the troops being used on D-Day being airborne insertions, it was essential that they were given adequate support and a special unit of the Royal Army Service Corps (RASC), the 716 (Airborne) Light Composite Company, was formed in 1943. A small contingent landed by glider on D-Day while others arrived by sea. Their task was to gather and distribute supplies to the units of the 6th Airborne Division. Among the unit's casualties suffered on D-Day was another

A Centaur IV Cruiser Tank of the Royal Marines 1st Armoured Support Group shortly after D-Day. (Public Domain)

Middlesbrough soldier. Driver John William Lunn was aged just 19 and left behind his parents, John William and Mary Ann Lunn.[10]

Pvt Albert Barker was a 24-year-old from Middlesbrough who was killed in action going ashore on Sword Beach with 1 Norfolk Regiment. He lies in La Deliverande War Cemetery in the small village of the same name, which lies just behind what were Oboe and Peter Sectors of Sword Beach.

When the names of those who had lost their lives on D-Day were tallied and assessed, it was almost inevitable that there would be some administrative errors. One which appears to have been fairly common, however, was the number of Royal Navy casualties who were classed as having been lost serving on HMS *Copra*. In fact HMS *Copra* was a shore establishment at Largs in Scotland which was responsible for processing pay and allowances for RN personnel serving in Combined Operations. Among these mislabelled casualties was a 19-year-old Middlesbrough sailor, Able Seaman Ben Nicholls, who was in all likelihood serving aboard a landing craft that was lost.[11]

The 50th (Northumbrian) Division had seen extensive action throughout the war and, unsurprisingly, went ashore in the first wave on D-Day. A component unit of the division was 6 Green Howards, a unit with strong Middlesbrough ties. Among those killed in the assault was Lance Corporal Francis Richard Cartwright, a 29-year-old married Middlesbrough man.[12] Also killed on D-Day was Sgt Frank Owens of 1 Hampshire Regiment. The 28-year-old Middlesbrough-native left behind his widow, Elizabeth (Betty) and two daughters, Pat and Ann.[13]

Middlesbrough received another royal visit on 26 July when the Princess Royal toured the town accompanied by her Lady-in-Waiting, the Dowager Lady Lloyd. The first visit on her itinerary was to inspect members of the ATS followed by a visit to the Mission for Seamen's Hostel. Welcomed by the Mayor (Councillor R. Ridley), the Princess said that she was pleased to think that the men of the Royal Navy and the Merchant Navy, along with the other services, could avail themselves of a hot meal and she wished the mission the very best of luck. The Princess spoke to several men who had experienced attacks on their ships by both U-Boats and aircraft; as she left, the seamen gave her three rousing cheers. The Princess concluded the visit by opening three new nurseries and offering congratulations to the authorities in Middlesbrough for providing facilities for children.

Although the cinema had played a vital role throughout the war, giving people relaxation and enjoyment as well as wartime information, not everyone was a fan. In August several Middlesbrough headmasters had criticised the effect it was having on young boys who they believed were less active and were attending the cinemas in the town far too frequently, to the detriment of their future development. They were joined by the headmaster of Guisborough Grammar School, R.J. Routh, who stated that it was his belief that cinema visits should be rationed as frequent 'visits to the kinema induced mental sluggishness'.[14]

Further development of ship types, informed by years of war experience, resulted in the creation of the innovative Loch-class anti-submarine warfare frigate, and Smith's Dock received several orders for vessels of this type. Although almost ninety were ordered nationally, the vast majority were cancelled at the end of the war and only six saw active service with the Royal Navy. Among them was HMS *Loch Eck* which was built and launched by Smith's in 1944 before being commissioned in early 1945. Despite her short service life, she went on to sink (or aid in sinking) three U-Boats and was also involved in the liberation and reoccupation of Norway at the end of the war.[15]

We have already heard how the twin Trowsdale brothers, in their capacities as Masters in the Merchant Navy, had been introduced to the King and Queen, but on 16 August tragedy struck the family when the young son of Wilfred (the brother who worked in the offices of the Constantine Shipping Company) and Minnie Thistle Trowsdale lost his life. Unsurprisingly in this seafaring family, 17-year-old Frederick William Trowsdale had joined the merchant service as an apprentice, but was lost when the unescorted SS *Empire Lancer* was torpedoed and sunk in the Mozambique Channel with the loss of forty-two of her seventy-nine crew.[16]

We earlier heard how the Hon. Colonel of the Green Howards had opened Middlesbrough's Salute the Soldier campaign in May. During his speech General Sir H.E. Franklyn had closed his remarks by telling the people of Middlesbrough that his son, Captain John Belfield Edmund Franklyn (22), was serving with the regiment's 6th Battalion. Just four months later Captain Franklyn was killed in action in the fighting around Arnhem.[17]

The final day of November was a bittersweet occasion for the men of the Home Guard as the day marked the final parades of the force in Middlesbrough, Stockton and the surrounding area. Thousands of Home Guards were on parade and, despite the weather, crowds turned out to cheer the men on.

CHAPTER 6

1945 – A Victorious Ending

On 1 March the Liberal MP for Middlesbrough West, Harcourt 'Crinks' Johnstone, died suddenly of a cerebral stroke aged just 49. This meant that Middlesbrough had to hold its second wartime by-election; once again, due to the wartime agreement, it would be unopposed. The candidate for the Liberal Party raised eyebrows as it was none other than Air Vice-Marshal Don Bennett, DSO, at the time the commanding officer of 8 (Pathfinder) Group of RAF Bomber Command. The tough Australian had established a reputation as one of the most brilliant airmen and commanders in the RAF and was very widely respected by many. His political ambitions were already known, but there was some surprise as his previous attempt in 1944 to be selected as a candidate had

Air Vice-Marshall Don Bennett, DSO. Elected as MP for Middlesbrough West. (Public Domain)

been for the Conservative Party.[1] Bennett, largely because of the unopposed nature of the election, became MP for Middlesbrough West on 14 May, just days after VE Day.

By the end of the war, Dorman Long & Co. had managed to make a massive contribution to the war effort. During the course of the war the firm turned out 6.5 million tons of metal ingots, mined more than 16 million tons of coal alongside 8.75 million tons of ironstone and over 1.5 million tons of limestone. One of its construction shops had been fitted for the mass production of floating bridgework and the construction of Bailey bridges which proved so useful in many theatres of war. In its by-products plants, the company had produced benzine fuel, anthracene which was used in the creation of khaki dye and toluene used in explosives.

Harcourt 'Crinks' Johnstone, MP. (Public Domain)

The Dorman Long subsidiary, Tees Side Bridge & Engineering Works Ltd, had also made a massive contribution during a war in which its workers had laboured non-stop. During the course of the war the company had manufactured a massive variety of metal items. These included air raid shelters, aircraft hangars, bridges, tank turrets, armoured cars, and power stations, and its shipyards produced craft including gunboats, rocket-firing craft (mainly for use in the Far East) and a variety of landing craft. By the time construction had ended in 1944 the company had produced and launched 214 landing craft, thirty gunboats and forty-eight rocket-firing craft.

F. Hills and Son Ltd., during the course of the war, produced 480,000 Jablo aircraft propeller blades, millions of strips of 'Window', 812 Percival Proctor trainer and communications aircraft, and 13,500 trailing edges for the wings of Avro Anson aircraft. The company's greatest contribution, however, was probably the more than 10 million sq ft of aeronautical plywood which it produced, the majority of which, over 6 million sq ft, went into the production of the De Haviland Mosquito aircraft.

With dawn on 8 May the people of Middlesbrough were met with the news that the war in Europe was indeed over. Many had heard the news late the night before and large groups had celebrated into the early hours before retiring for a few hours sleep. Germany had surrendered unconditionally and nearly six years of European conflict were finally over. The atmosphere that morning was undoubtedly one of celebration, but it was tinged with regret and loss. Many families in the Middlesbrough area had lost loved ones in the war and many others had family members still at risk serving in the fight against Japan. To some, celebrating seemed somehow inappropriate.

Nevertheless, the scenes on the streets were undoubtedly busier as people tried desperately to secure food supplies for the street parties and festivities to come. In residential streets women and children (joined by men who were not serving) hurriedly made preparations, putting up bunting and flags, preparing bonfires and effigies (Hitler was by far the most popular) and putting out what furniture they could to host the coming street party while others toiled in kitchens preparing sandwiches and other treats (mainly to be consumed by the children).

One of the most popular and common themes for the celebrations was the fancy dress competition for local children. While the street party and dances were the most common forms of celebration, there were others. A parade of the civil defence services was quickly organised and held while others preferred more sombre and calm reflections and visited church services or went to the open-air service that was held in Albert Park. Many pubs also had a busy day, but a beer shortage meant that many were forced to close early.

In Stockton people took to the streets almost as soon as the news broke and bonfires were quickly started. People who had already gone to bed heard the commotion and, finding out the reason, immediately threw on clothes and took to the street to begin the celebrations. Despite it being the early hours, hundreds were soon thronging the streets and dancing and singing were commonplace as rockets and other fireworks lit the night sky. Ships berthed in the Tees took up the celebrations by sounding their hooters and sirens.

There were similar scenes of jubilation in Thornaby. Here, the celebrations in the early hours were led by a group of airmen, one of whom blew on a bugle, while others banged dustbin lids as they marched through the streets. They were quickly joined by hundreds of civilians and service personnel who made their way toward Stockton to join the partying there. Once again, bonfires were quickly assembled and lit, with people consigning everything from furniture, clothing and doors torn from coal cellars to the flames.

Meanwhile, at Orwell Street there was a crisis. Twins had just been born into the Gamesby family that morning, but the baby girls weighed only a combined 7lbs; the doctor had offered little hope and advised the family to let nature take its course. Thankfully, the grandfather of the newborn twins (Henry) had other ideas, advising the family not to wash them but to clean them with oil, massage their lungs and keep their mouths clear. Henry was a St John's volunteer ambulanceman and the twins were also fortunate that their grandmother also had a talent for caring for children. Thankfully, Pamela Clare and Victoria May Gamesby not only survived but thrived, and the birth on VE Day attracted media attention. As night came in bonfires were lit and fireworks were set off.

Stoneyhurst Avenue, North Ormesby, children's fancy dress competition.
(Evening Gazette)

Street party on Sutton Estate. (Evening Gazette)

Street party in Warwick Street. (Evening Gazette)

For James Henry and Dorothy Brown the end of the European war must have come as a relief as they had at least one son serving in the Army. Tragedy, however, was to strike. Pvt Frederick Brown had joined the Border Regiment but was serving as part of the 1st Airborne when

Another view of the Warwick Street party. (Evening Gazette)

VE Day on Rushford Street. (Evening Gazette)

the battalion was sent to Norway to disarm the remaining German garrison forces. During the landing of the 1st Airborne, however, an air crash resulted in the loss of several lives, Pvt Frederick Brown was one of those killed on 10 May, two days after Germany surrendered.

Children celebrating at Haverton Hill. (Evening Gazette)

Carlton Street Party. (Evening Gazette)

Following VE Day there was an anticipation of a sharp decline in the wartime shipbuilding boom but in the immediate months after the end of the war in Europe, Smith's Dock was kept busy working on armed

Skinner Street, Stockton, on VE Day. (Evening Gazette)

NFS parade on Linthorpe Road on VE Day. (Evening Gazette)

Malvern Road, Billingham. (Evening Gazette)

VE Day service at Albert Park. (Evening Gazette)

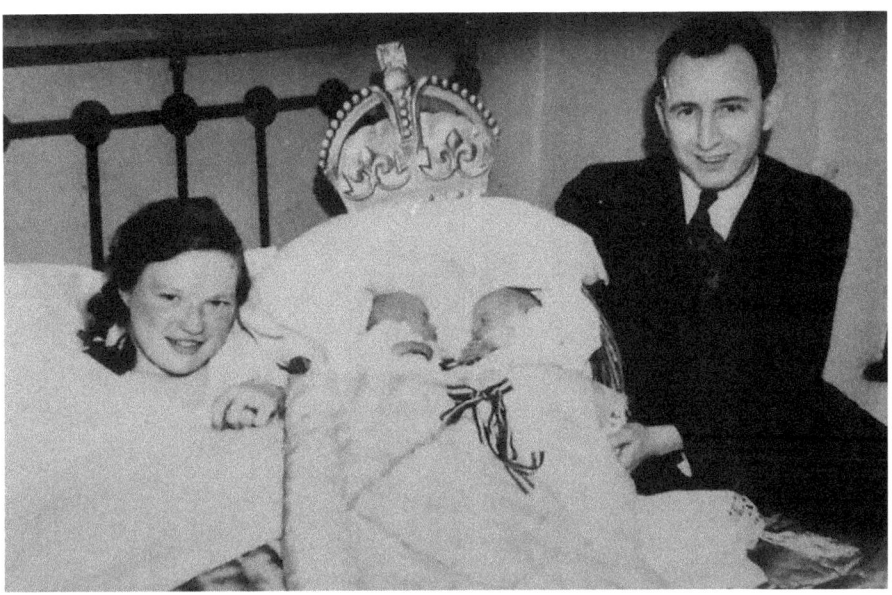

The Gamesby family with their VE Day arrivals. (Evening Gazette)

trawlers, converting them back for peacetime use to ensure that food supplies could be maintained in Britain.

A general election coincided with the end of the war in Europe and the Labour landslide which followed, including on Teesside, was a clear indicator that although the people of the area (and the country) had been firmly behind the war effort, they also wished for a change in British society. A key factor in the victory, especially in working-class areas, was the promise of the Labour government to create a more caring society, including a National Health Service. The general election saw Labour make great gains across Teesside. For one MP the election brought an unwelcome fame. The newly elected MP for Middlesbrough West, Air Vice-Marshal Don Bennett, DSO, became one of the shortest serving MPs when he was defeated by the Labour Party candidate, Geoffrey Cooper, by 2,613 votes in the election. His tenure as MP had lasted just seventy-three days.[2]

Despite VE Day, the war in the East went on with many men from the Middlesbrough area still serving. Among them was Flight Sergeant

William Nattrass, a 21-year-old pilot with 84 Squadron. At the time the squadron was re-equipping with the Mosquito and was practising dive-bombing techniques in anticipation of supporting operations against the Japanese mainland. On 14 May, Nattrass and his navigator took off from RAF Chharra for a practice flight but their Mosquito VI (HR628) was seen to break up while in a dive and both airmen were killed.[3]

The day following the death of F/Sgt Nattrass, another Middlesbrough serviceman lost his life. Pvt Alfred Kenneth Robinson (21) of 2 West Yorks was killed in action fighting against the Japanese forces in Burma.[4]

The fighting against the Japanese continued and although Burma was retaken there was much anxiety over the losses that would be suffered in any invasion of Japan itself. The dropping of two atomic bombs (which in different circumstances might have been developed on Teesside) over the cities of Hirsohima and Nagasaki, however, brought about a swift end to the war and once more the people of Teesside awoke to a two-day victory celebration; this time for the end of the war. The celebrations were of a similar nature to those which had been experienced on VE Day but the atmosphere was, indeed, more muted.

Members of the Boys' Brigade celebrate VE Day at Croft. (Northern Echo)

It seemed that the victory over Japan was not as warmly celebrated as that over Germany had been.

Nevertheless, there were celebrations and street parties, as well as the now familiar dances, fireworks and bonfires. At Croft, some 200 boys from the South Durham Battalion of the Boys' Brigade were in camp when the news broke. The lads, from Stockton, Thornaby, Norton, Billingham, and Eaglescliffe, celebrated with gusto and joined in the fun in Croft before they returned home to their families.

Endnotes

Chapter 1: 1939 – The Coming of the Storm

1. HMS *Courageous* had begun life as a Courageous-class cruiser and had been launched in 1916 before taking part in the final two years of the First World War. Due to naval treaty rules she was converted into an aircraft carrier with the work being complete by 1928.
2. *North Eastern Gazette*, 22 September 1939, p. 8.
3. Boy 1st Class Willard is commemorated on the Portsmouth Naval Memorial.
4. Engine Room Artificer 4th Class Blenkiron is commemorated on the Portsmouth Naval Memorial.
5. OS Heslop is commemorated on the Portsmouth Naval Memorial.
6. OS Trenholm is commemorated on the Portsmouth Naval Memorial.
7. All three men are commemorated on the Tower Hill Memorial.

Chapter 2: 1940 – A Year of Trials

1. Bower was a contentious figure. In 1938 he had been involved in a heated Commons debate with Jewish Labour MP Emmanuel Shinwell. As a result of Shinwell alleging him of lying he had told the Jewish MP to 'go back to Poland', at which point Shinwell had crossed the floor and struck him in the face.
2. *Yorkshire Post*, 6 February 1940, p. 1.
3. The vast majority of men lost on the *Exmouth* were never recovered. Eighteen bodies were later found by a truant schoolboy on a beach near Wick.
4. AS Lowery is commemorated on the Portsmouth Naval Memorial.

5. Interestingly, a Crosthwaite owned tug company on the Tyne too; Joseph Crosthwaite Tugs Ltd was based in North Shields but there was apparently no family connection between the two.

6. Mr Liddle is commemorated on the Tower Hill Memorial.

7. Both men are buried at Middlesbrough (Linthorpe) Cemetery.

8. Both of these young sailors are commemorated on the Tower Hill Memorial.

9. *North Eastern Gazette*, 9 February 1940, p. 5.

10. There is some confusion over P/O Burrell. The CWGC claims that he was a cricketer for Middlesex CCC but there is no mention elsewhere of this. Some online sources claim that P/O Burrell was killed in a flying accident, but his death certificate shows that his death occurred over the North Sea and that the cause of death was a bullet wound through the head. This clearly shows that P/O Burrell was the pilot of the Anson on that ill-fated day.

11. Mr Brown is buried at Amble West Cemetery.

12. Stoker Stephenson is commemorated on the Chatham Naval Memorial.

13. The battalion had a particularly unlucky first three years of war. Following its bad luck in France it was later taken prisoner en-masse during the Battle of Gazala in June 1942.

14. Both Pvts Chandler and Henry survived their captivity. Pvt Henry remained in the Army and, as of 1948, was still serving in the Green Howards.

15. Gnr Askey is commemorated on the Dunkirk Memorial.

16. Pvt Newton is commemorated on the Dunkirk Memorial.

17. Tpr Orton is buried at Dozinghem Military Cemetery.

18. Mr Crackles lies in Middlesbrough (Linthorpe) Cemetery. The MV *Beal* went on to have a long and interesting career during which she changed names a further five times. At the end of the war she was renamed the *Sylvian Coast*, transferred to a Glaswegian company in 1959 she was renamed the *Lairdsburn*, she was then sold to a Greek company and renamed the *Agia Sofia* in 1966 before changing

hands once more in 1975 and being renamed the *Friendship III* before changing hands for the last time in 1976 and renamed the *Ariadne*. It was in this guise, three years later, that she met her end, sinking after striking the breakwater at Augusta while on a voyage between Cephalonia and Barcelona.

19. Stoker Byrne is commemorated on the Plymouth Naval Memorial.
20. All three men are commemorated on the Lowestoft Naval Memorial.
21. Mrs Scollen's two previous husbands (Jack Young and Ralph Brown) had both died in tragic accidents at the North Skelton Ironstone Mine.
22. *North Eastern Gazette*, 8 November 1940, p. 3.
23. OS Barnard is commemorated on the Tower Hill Memorial.
24. Supply Assistant Harper is commemorated on the Portsmouth Naval Memorial.
25. Stoker Richardson is commemorated on the Portsmouth Naval Memorial.

Chapter 4: 1942 – A Year of Loss

1. *Perthshire Advertiser*, 3 June 1942, p. 5.
2. *Newcastle Journal*, 19 June 1942, p. 1.

Chapter 5: 1943–1944 – Attrition

1. During the course of the war six Victoria Crosses were awarded to PIAT operators.
2. *London Gazette*, 6 July 1943, p. 3095.
3. The SS *Empire Chieftain* was sold at the end of the war to Royal Mail Lines and renamed the SS *Loch Ryan*. She served until 1960 when she was broken up in Japan.
4. The *Empire Law* became the RFA *Wave Conquerer* while the *Empire Bounty* became the RFA *Wave Victor*. The first-named served in Korea and was scrapped in 1960 while the *Wave Victor*

also served well in the RFA before being transferred to the RAF as a refuelling hulk at RAF Gan. She was then laid up in 1975 but not finally scrapped until 1981.

5. *Newcastle Journal*, 9 February 1944, p. 3.

6. *Yorkshire Post*, 15 May 1944, p., 1.

7. Pvt Dresser was serving with the 7th Green Howards when he was awarded the VC for an action on 17 May 1917 while Major Cooper, then a Sgt, had been serving with the 12th King's Royal Rifle Corps when he was awarded the VC for an action at Passchendaele on 16 August 1917.

8. Newcastle Journal, 16 May 1944, p. 1.

9. Marine Bennison is buried at Dannes Communal Cemetery.

10. Dvr Lunn is buried in Ranville War Cemetery.

11. AS Nicholls' body was never recovered and he is commemorated on the Portsmouth Naval Memorial.

12. L/Cpl Cartwright's body rests in Bayeux War Cemetery.

13. Sgt Owens lies in Bayeux War Cemetery.

14. *Kinematograph Weekly*, 10 August 1944, p. 19.

15. HMS *Loch Eck* went on to be transferred to the Royal New Zealand Navy in 1948 and was renamed as the HMNZS *Walea*. She served in the Korean War before being put into reserve in 1957 and was scrapped in the mid-1960s.

16. Mr Trowsdale is commemorated on the Tower Hill Memorial.

17. Captain Franklyn had been wounded two months earlier. He is buried at Arnhem Oosterbeek Cemetery. His headstone bears the inscription : 'SON AND GRANDSON OF GREEN HOWARDS, BOTH COLONELS OF THE REGIMENT'. Captain Franklyn was registered as living on the Isle of Man.

Chapter 6: 1945 – A Victorious Ending

1. Bennett had been narrowly defeated in his campaign for candidature by none other than Wing Commander Guy Gibson, VC, DSO and

Bar, DFC and Bar. Gibson had resigned his candidature in August 1944 citing the demands of his RAF service but was killed in action just a month later.

2. Bennett was the only Bomber Command Group commanding officer not to be given a knighthood at the end of the war. He resigned his commission and became involved in the aviation and motoring industries. He continued to harbour political ambitions but was unsuccessful in three election attempts (in 1948, 1950 and 1967). During the 1970s he threw his support behind several fringe far-right parties and in the 1974 general election he stood under an anti-EEC banner against the incumbent Conservative PM, Edward Heath, but finished last with just 1.5 per cent of the vote. Don Bennett died, aged 76, on 15 September (Battle of Britain Day) 1986.

3. F/Sgt Nattrass is buried at Ranchi War Cemetery.

4. Pvt Robinson is buried at Rangoon War Cemetery.

Index